The Vatican's Exorcists

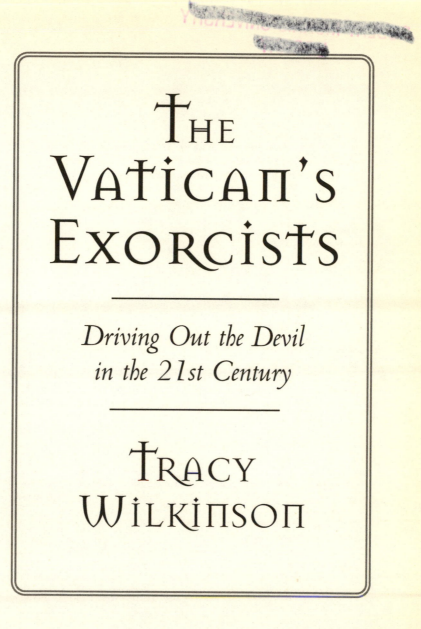

†HE VA†ICAN'S EXORCIS†S

Driving Out the Devil
in the 21st Century

†RACY WILKINSON

Warner Books
Hachette Book Group USA
1271 Avenue of the Americas
New York, NY 10020

Visit our Web site at www.HachetteBookGroupUSA.com.

Printed in the United States of America

First Edition: February 2007
10 9 8 7 6 5 4 3 2 1

Warner Books and the "W" logo are trademarks of Time Warner Inc. or an affiliated company. Used under license by Hachette Book Group USA, which is not affiliated with Time Warner Inc.

Library of Congress Cataloging-in-Publication Data

Wilkinson, Tracy.
    The Vatican's exorcists : driving out the devil in the 21st century / Tracy Wilkinson.
— 1st ed.
        p. cm.
    ISBN-13: 978-0-446-57885-1
    ISBN-10: 0-446-57885-1
    1. Exorcism. 2. Catholic Church—Doctrines. 3. Amorth, Gabriele. I. Title.
    BX2340.W55 2007
    264'.020994—dc22   2006019195

Book design by Giorgetta Bell McRee

To Mike.

Acknowledgments

My experience as a journalist has more to do with wars, guerrilla movements, and political conflict than with ancient rituals of the planet's largest religion. But my years in Rome have immersed me in this world of faith and devotion, and taught me to respect a system of beliefs that sometimes seems foreign.

This book was written in the spirit of attempting to understand that which is mystifying. I am grateful to the many priests, psychiatrists, patients, and others who agreed to speak to me for this project.

There are many other people whom I'd like to thank: journalists John Allen and Cindy Wooden for helping me navigate the corridors of the Vatican and the intricacies of the religion; Tod Tamberg of the Los Angeles archdiocese for the discussion on ways to view evil; and Father

Keith Pecklers of Rome's Pontifical Gregorian University for reading pages and generally enlightening me on the teachings and workings of the Catholic Church. There are also officials at the Vatican, whose names I cannot mention, whose assistance was critical.

In the secular world, Scott Lilienfeld, a professor of psychology at Emory University in Atlanta, provided crucial insight on how the human mind works and pointed the way in research of this field.

Among my most direct collaborators, I must thank Nancy Meiman for accompanying me on my very first meeting with Father Amorth, and Pietro de Cristofaro, who, with persistence, established invaluable contacts in the pursuit of exorcists. Plus, he knows Latin.

Colleague Livia Borghese deserves special recognition; we embarked on a wonderful road trip that resulted in critical interviews and access.

And endless appreciation goes to my husband, Mike O'Connor, whose support sustained me to the end.

Finally, there is one person without whom this book would not be possible. Maria de Cristofaro identified the trend of exorcisms and saw the potential for a good story long before I did. It was her belief in the topic that kept this project alive, and it was her guidance that carried it each step of the way.

Any errors and misjudgments are my own.

Contents

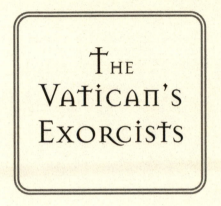

The Vatican's Exorcists

PROLOGUE

Caterina seems the picture of normalcy. Tall, blue-eyed, and blond, the forty-five-year-old Italian woman has the slender, taut body of the professional dancer she is. She comes from a good family, the daughter of a surgeon and a music teacher. She speaks calmly and intelligently, not an intellectual but a person with education and grace.

Her exorcist is Father Efrem Cirlini of Bologna.

At seventy-nine years of age, Father Efrem is one of the oldest of Italy's approximately 350 exorcists. He looks a bit like Santa Claus, a man with a full, bushy white beard who cuts a rotund figure under his rough-hewn tan cassock. He wears a thick leather belt around his ample waist and a tiny wooden cross pinned to the left side of his chest. Caterina and Efrem have been meeting weekly for years, sometimes just for prayer, and sometimes for what both describe as a full-blown exorcism of the demons that possess this troubled woman.

An authentic exorcism, like psychotherapy, is not a one-shot deal. It can take many, many attempts to banish the devil. What happens in Italy, in numerous Catholic churches, is a Vatican-sanctioned ritual involving people who truly believe. This is not Hollywood.

On a hot late summer morning, Caterina and Efrem met for one of their sessions. It was a Friday, and these appointments are as much a part of Caterina's schedule as going to the dentist or teaching one of her dance classes. She stepped casually through the heavy wooden doors of the sixteenth-century Ss. Gregorio e Siro Church, on a back street in central Bologna, where Father Efrem practices. Outside, Smart cars and motorbikes pushed through a city as famous for its communist governments as its renaissance architecture, with buildings the color of terra cotta. Inside, elderly women dressed all in black whispered prayers at small hushed chapels and lit devotional candles. Modernity and tradition, two worlds seemingly as different as could be. And yet here they do not collide, they intersect. A contemporary Bolognan seeks help in an ancient ritual.

Father Efrem and Caterina began solemnly and rhythmically with prayers and blessings. But within minutes Caterina transformed into another soul, at times angry, at times mournful, emitting voices from some unknown place deep in her body and bone-chilling screams that echoed under the vaulted ceilings of a side room inside the cavernous medieval church.

"Padre nostro, che sei nei cieli, sia santificato il tuo nome," they recited at first, in unison. "Our Father who art in heaven, hallowed be thy name . . ."

Caterina sat in a green plastic chair in the center of the room. The tools of the exorcism were laid out on a large oval wooden table to one side: the red book of rites and prayers; a silver crucifix; a bottle of holy water from Lourdes, and a small plastic canister of holy oil. Efrem lifted and placed a purple satin stole around his neck, then stood off to Caterina's right side. Her eyes darted around the room, finally focusing on a distant point. She worked her right thumb against her left hand, rubbing, kneading, worrying.

"Ave Maria, full of grace. . . . Holy Mary, Mother of God, pray for us sinners now and at the hour of our death. . . ."

Efrem moved behind Caterina, placed his hands on her head, and then anointed her forehead, making the sign of the cross with holy oil. It is these blatantly religious symbols that most pester the devil, say priests. Immediately Caterina's face contorted, her cheeks flushed. Efrem pressed on, making signs of the cross on each hand and the nape of her neck. She grimaced, as if in pain. Her voice suddenly became weak and raspy, even as she continued to attempt to recite a prayer. "Gesù Cristo! Jesus Christ!" Then her body convulsed violently, a seizure wringing her lanky frame.

"I can't do it!" she boomed in a voice deeper than what seemed possible. Repeatedly she exhaled air, blowing through her lips almost comically, like a child blowing bubbles, and as if she were expelling inner toxic fumes. She shook her head back and forth, back and forth.

Alternately, her normal voice returned, then other voices emerged: the hoarse, laryngitis voice; a little girl voice; and most dramatically, the deep masculine voice. At times, she even spoke of herself using masculine verb conjugations and pronouns. It was, Efrem explained later, the devil himself speaking.

Alarmed but persistent, Father Efrem placed a large crucifix against her throat. "Pray for us!" he implored to a litany of saints. "Saint Michael, pray for us. Saint Gabriel, pray for us. Saint Raphael, pray for us." Caterina attempted to push the cross away and rolled her eyes in disgust. Her violent reactions surged when the priest uttered the name of John Paul II, the late pope. She clasped her head, then hurled forward. Each time the priest removed the cross, she lost her voice again, choking. "Signore pietà. Lord, have pity!" Efrem cried. "Free us, oh Lord!" Suddenly, Caterina began emitting groans that sounded like a monster vomiting. Over and over. She sat ramrod erect in the green chair, her hands frozen into claws. "This is foul!" she growled, huffing. "Basta stupido prete! Enough, you stupid priest!"

Father Efrem stepped away and retrieved the thin red book containing the exorcism rites. Clutching the crucifix in his right hand, he crossed himself three times, on the forehead, lips, and left side of his chest. He moved behind Caterina again, touched her head, and began to read the exorcism prayer. She closed her eyes, then her face contorted. The bones of her face were more pronounced, her aspect more gaunt. She wrung her hands together relentlessly.

"Basta gia!" she moaned, stamping her foot. "I can't take this anymore! Basta gia, prete!"

"Renounce Satan!" Efrem intoned. "Renounce the seduction of evil! Renounce Satan!"

"No!" Caterina called back. "No! No! No!"

Then, shaking her head, her index finger raised to her lips, she hissed, "Shhhhhhh!"

"Do you believe in God?" Efrem demanded. Caterina struggled to respond. She stamped her foot again, grabbed her head, and exhaled heavily. In the tiniest, barely audible voice, she muttered, "I believe."

"Do you believe in Jesus Christ?" Efrem again demanded.

She cringed, closed her eyes tightly, opened them, and focused high on the ceiling. Again, a voice fighting to be heard said, "I believe."

Quickly Efrem launched into another round of "Our Father who art in heaven." Caterina's body twitched as the priest prayed over her. "Please, please, enough!" she cried. "Sono stufo! I am fed up with this! Basta, prete!" He placed his purple stole over her right shoulder, and she lurched forward and screamed, "Basta!" She then froze in pain, her head slowly shaking back and forth.

Standing behind her, he held the stole in place with his right hand. In his left hand he held the crucifix, which he touched to her left shoulder. He bent over her head as if to embrace her with his body.

"Ti comando, Satana! I command you, Satan! Leave Caterina, servant of God!"

She leaned forward, her face again an ugly mask of pain. The monster again vomited, long, harsh, guttural screams of anguish from deep inside a tortured soul.

"Leave this creature! Vattene, Satana! Be gone, Satan!" The priest forced the crucifix against her back. Her head was in her hands. The screams reverberated again and again, each longer and more horrific than the one before it.

Finally Caterina fell backwards in her chair, her body now limp. "Enough, enough," she muttered. Then her body lunged forward again and she screamed. She twisted her body to try to push the cross away from her back. She screamed and screamed. Efrem repeated: "Be gone, Satan!"

A scream even deeper than the earlier ones thundered from Caterina: "You stupid priest! Enough, you cretin!" Suddenly, a little girl's voice followed: "Stop, please, I beg you, stop," she said amid pitiful sobs. Caterina cried and moaned, and Efrem continued to pray. She doubled forward. "I didn't want to come here, I didn't want to. It's your fault. I hate you!"

The priest wiped her tears, but she pushed him away. As he prayed softly, her body, first her legs, then her torso, twitched. She grimaced, and a stronger, harsher voice returned: "Die, priest! Die, priest! Die, priest! Die, priest!"

"Holy Mary, Mother of God, pray for us sinners now and at the hour of our death," Efrem prayed and turned to the next rite, one of healing.

"Heal us, oh Lord! Heal her, oh Lord!"

Caterina abruptly went erect and slid from the chair. "Leave me alone, priest," she said. "She will never heal! It is useless. Go away! She will never heal!"

The voice from Caterina continued in a singsong taunt of the priest: "She will never heal! She will never heal! She will never heal!"

Efrem was breathless by now, growing weary of the battle. He repeated the prayer of healing. "Heal her, oh Lord! Pray for us!"

"No, no, no!" the voice from Caterina responded. She jerked upright again in the chair. The moaning resumed, but now a bit softer. She seemed to calm. Slowly, she recited a prayer in unison with Efrem.

"Are you alright now?" he asked her. She motioned with her head: more or less.

Efrem sang a chant in the ancient language of Latin. Caterina wept, but quietly, more of relief than anguish. Briefly her body again contorted, but Efrem placed his hands on her shoulders and she grew calm. He touched her with the purple stole and intoned the litany of saints to ask for their prayers.

Caterina brightened. She announced that she was "eighty percent" better. She retied her long blond ponytail and clasped hands with Efrem, who recited another prayer. She joined in easily. She looked straight ahead, then up at her priest. The ordeal was over.

Suddenly, the sky outside clouded over, the room inside went dark.

Panicked, Caterina grabbed the sides of her chair and, still seated, pushed herself backwards a good six feet across the floor. "No! No! No! No!" she shouted in a deep voice. She cried and rocked her head back and forth, beating her fists against the chair. "I told you no!"

Efrem rushed his stole around her shoulders and launched anew into prayer. A creaky, old person's voice came from Caterina. "Stop it! I said no! I can't take it anymore," the voice pleaded.

After a few more minutes of prayer, Caterina calmed down and grew still. Efrem whispered to her that she should now feel better. Slowly, she smiled. Yes, now it was truly over.

Outside, the sun came out again, bathing the room in light.

CHAPTER 1

Introduction

From its very first days, the Roman Catholic Church has formally sanctioned exorcisms with enthusiasm that has varied through the centuries—sometimes promoting the ritual overtly, and during other periods, appearing to be embarrassed by it. Jesus Christ performed exorcisms more than 2,000 years ago, according to the Bible, as did his more recent vicar, Pope John Paul II. Believers see the exorcism as a major battle of wills between God and the superior forces of good on one side and evil on the other.

An exorcism is a ritual in which prayer is used to banish the devil, demons, or satanic spirits from a person or place. It is most familiar to Americans through popular culture, through movies like the 1973 horror classic *The Exorcist*, based on William Peter Blatty's novel, and its sequels and various knockoffs. Most Americans probably associate the ceremonial flailing and screaming in darkened rooms amid chanting and bizarre, supernatural antics with rogue clerics or Holy Roller evangelists.

In fact, the procedure is accepted, sanctioned, and performed selectively, but far more commonly than one would expect, as part of Catholic doctrine and especially in Roman Catholic Italy. Many Italian priests and devout Catholics believe in the power of a force known as the devil or demons to vex, possess, and lead astray otherwise normal people. And they believe in the power of prayer to cast him (or it or them) aside. Exorcism comes from the Greek word for *oath*. An exorcism can be as simple as a prayer, a blessing; or, more rarely, it can be a more dramatic, sometimes violent ritual. It remains, nevertheless, controversial, a phenomenon that is mysterious and anachronistic to the outside world, and one that has many detractors within the Church as well.

No priest has done more to push exorcism into the mainstream than Rome's Father Gabriele Amorth, arguably modern day's most famous exorcist. With Amorth as a starting point of reference, this book will examine the rite of exorcism in detail, its history, its decline, and its current revival. Yes, revival. The number of people performing and seeking exorcisms has grown significantly in Italy. We will examine the reasons for this, which range from the kind of promotional work Amorth has done to the endorsement of two popes, a political climate that personifies evil, and the rampant fears of a population increasingly alienated from its moral foundations.

A debate also persists within the Rome-based Church itself. Priests disagree on how to interpret and analyze the presence of evil and the nature of the devil in the world today. Exorcists disagree on style, conditions, and some of the very definitions that underpin their work. And the Church hierarchy, while defending the necessity and discreet appropriateness of exorcism, continues to harbor deep misgivings over the way it is sometimes practiced. Father Amorth and his very public discussion of exorcism drive some elements of the top Vatican leadership to distraction; they disapprove of his showmanship tendencies. Yet there is no centralized oversight: exorcists report to their bishops, and the amount of autonomy an exorcist has can vary from diocese to diocese. Many Church officials prefer to see this as a fringe issue, noting that those who perform exorcisms are a tiny fraction of the clergy. These priests and other Vatican officials cannot say demonic possession is an impossibility because it is contained in Church dogma. But they fear—with justification—that this uncomfortable topic will be misinterpreted and sensationalized. They would rather it not be highlighted at all, in deference to more positive, life-affirming aspects of the religion.

Evolving thought and concern over exaggeration has prompted the Vatican to slightly change the rules governing exorcism for the first time in several hundred years, in an effort to give a nod to advances in the understanding of medical science and to prevent abuse. We will examine the generational divide within the growing ranks of Italy's exorcists. The new crop, many of them inspired by Amorth, grapples with concerns about when exorcism is appropriate and whether it might do more harm than good in cases when it is not. Among these is Father Francois-Marie Dermine, the exorcist of Ancona, who thinks perhaps priests have failed in listening to their parishioners. And Father Gabriele Nanni, who manages to balance piety, fundamentalism, and fervent belief in the devil with a scholarly analysis of faith. Members of the older generation, including Amorth and Andrea Gemma, "the only bishop exorcist," take a more casual, almost cavalier attitude and chafe at the new rules and the on-again, off-again efforts by the Vatican to rein them in.

As conversations with these men reveal, the work of the exorcist is quite delicate, and it remains an unusual calling. Even in Italy, where more people than anywhere else are willing to assume the mantle, the Church says there is a shortage of exorcists who can attend to the thousands of Italians who seek this kind of help. We will look at the somewhat clouded perspective of patients who have spent years with exorcists and also the question of why so many patients are women.

It is also important that the scientific community weigh in, and the attitude there is not as monolithic as one might expect. Certainly many psychologists and medical doctors rail against this practice as primitive and archaic. They challenge the notion of demonic possession in its very essence and say most characteristics displayed by the afflicted can be attributed to hysteria, unconscious role-playing, and high suggestibility on the part of patients. Exorcisms, contend the critics, are a hoax; the procedure is downright dangerous. Failure to discern serious illness, and instead, attributing it to the work of the devil, has led to death in a small number of exorcisms over the years, most notably in the United States and other parts of Europe. And yet there are men and women of science, particularly in Roman Catholic Italy, who are more accepting of the possibility of demonic possession, however rare it might be, and who see a role for prayer and the exorcist. "Science can't explain everything," says Salvatore di Salvo, a psychiatrist in the northern city of Turin.

I have approached this topic as a journalist, reserving my own analysis for specific moments and instead allowing exorcists and their patients to describe at length the phenomenon as they see it. I attended Caterina's exorcism and spent considerable time with her in her day-to-day life. I was allowed to listen to another exorcism that I describe later in the book. With two invaluable colleagues, Maria de Cristofaro and Livia Borghese, I conducted dozens of interviews with priests, psychologists, and historians. I do not attempt to judge the exorcists or their patients, or the Roman Catholic Church. However, the use of exorcisms and, more important, the growing number of Italians who think they need them raise troubling questions about society, organized religion, and mental health, questions that ultimately must be confronted.

Exorcism would seem in every way to conflict with the modern secular world, a world that is both fascinated and repelled by the phenomenon. It also generates conflict within the Church and even among those who practice it.

In the Blatty novel *The Exorcist*, the desperate mother Chris MacNeil seeks out Jesuit Father Damien Karras, who is also a psychiatrist, and asks him how she can find someone to perform an exorcism for a victim who she says is possessed. Chris has not yet revealed to Karras that the victim is her daughter. The Jesuit, an intellectual, is flabbergasted and responds dismissively, "Well, first you'd have to put him in a time machine and get him back to the sixteenth century."[1]

In fact, they had only to come to Italy.

CHAPTER II

Overview

The devil doesn't like Latin.

That is one of the first things I learned from Father Gabriele Amorth, long known as Rome's chief exorcist, even though that has never exactly been his formal title. Perhaps Rome's chattiest exorcist is the more apt title. Now past the age of eighty, Amorth has dedicated the last decades of his life to regaining a measure of respectability for exorcism. Despite his advancing age, he continues to perform the rite several times a week at his office in Rome. Scores of people seek him out. He prefers to use Latin when he conducts exorcisms, he says, because it is most effective in challenging the devil.

A little over a decade ago, Amorth founded the International Association of Exorcists, which holds a secret exorcists' convention in Italy every two years. He is the group's president emeritus. On alternate years, the national association of exorcists meets, also with Amorth in attendance. At the meeting in 2005, held in Todi in the Umbrian hills north of Rome, about 120 exorcists and other priests met to exchange ideas, stories about their cases, and tips on how to handle the delicate task they have undertaken. A handful of laywomen who often assist in exorcisms were also present. (In another sign of the Vatican's ambivalence, the association does not have official backing from the Congregation for Divine Worship, the division of the Vatican responsible for how rites like exorcism are conducted.)

Father Amorth knows most of the people at the conventions; he has had a hand in recruiting, training, or inspiring many of today's exorcists. In Italy the number of exorcists has, remarkably, grown tenfold in the last decade, by Amorth's count. As he slows his pace ever so slightly—old age and the rigors of a strenuous vocation catching up to him—he has overseen a new generation of exorcists and helped fuel a global renaissance of the ritual. "Devil detox" these days is something of a growth industry: in a world awash in catastrophe and unspeakable suffering, many people feel increasingly compelled to see evil in concrete and personified—not to mention simplified—forms, and to find a way to banish the bad.

For many troubled people, believing in the devil as something real and present helps explain today's tragedy and chaos. A prayer ritual that gets rid of him offers hope.

But how is evil defined and conceptualized? Is evil, as many people believe, merely the absence of good—*privatio boni*—a metaphysical concept? Or is evil a force, a physical entity, that acts? Is evil personal or impersonal? Is the devil a symbol or something concrete and real? It is this latter view of evil that is held by many priests and other Catholics for whom exorcism is an acceptable practice, because if evil is an active force, there must be a remedy, a way to combat it.

As is most obvious in the United States, but also in Europe, the belief in incarnate evil is especially strong among conservative Christians and fundamentalists, factions that are growing in number and clout. They have become the neocons of modern religion. Their way of thinking suggests a more literal interpretation of the Bible and a stark, less nuanced worldview that has been encouraged not just from pulpits but also from certain seats of world power. In the United States, a Harris Poll in December 2005 found that a stunning 60 percent of respondents believed in hell and the devil.[1] In the fifth century, Augustine and his peers found it useful to warn of the treacheries of the devil to scare followers into obedience; it was a form of political control. Some elements of organized religion today—notably American Pentecostals and the Catholic Charismatic movement—similarly use fear of a real, potent devil to whip up support and command loyal followings.[2] For them, the devil is making a big comeback.

Catholicism is an institution that claims to have central universal themes shared by more than a billion adherents, and that is true. But it is also a religion of great complexity, rolled out across many centuries and many continents and fed today by many different ways of dealing with the difficult.

Priests and devout Catholics cannot reject the possibility of demonic possession and practice of exorcism outright because to do so would go against scripture that enshrines the personification of evil. But they can and do diverge widely on what kind of emphasis should be placed on these themes. Fundamentalists and traditionalists are more inclined to conceive of a God who intervenes directly in the world. And if they believe in God's miraculous intervention, then they are also more inclined to believe in intervention, action, by the devil, a concrete evil force.

Liberals in the Church do not renounce belief in the reality of evil, but they are more likely to blame personal choice and look to individual responsibility. Where the conservatives cleave to the Bible's traditional language and literal reading of scripture, the liberals favor reinterpretation. Evil is more subtle, less spectacular, unexpected.

Many critics, however, see the Church's willingness to use exorcisms at all as a perilous crutch. It allows people to take flight from personal responsibility and constitutes not just a willful ignorance of serious mental illness but also, potentially, an exacerbation of such illness. Where psychiatry and therapy require a person to look within to solve his or her problems, exorcism and blaming the devil allows a person to escape introspection and instead discern only external causes for problems.

But Amorth and other practitioners quickly dismiss the criticism.

"Exorcism is God's true miracle," Amorth likes to say. And, he believes, it is a perfectly natural, spiritual reaction and attitude that crosses cultures.

"We of the Bible know that evil spirits are angels created as good by God and who then rebelled against God," Amorth said during one of our chats at the Society of Saint Paul congregational residence in suburban Rome, where, in a back room, he conducts exorcisms. "But the idea of evil spirits is a universal idea, in all cultures, all religions, all times. Naturally, everybody defends themselves according to their own culture and mentality . . . perhaps resorting to witch doctors or what have you. But all people, all the time, have a perception that spirits of evil exist, from which it is necessary to protect against."

Italy is a country steeped in its Catholic religiosity. Even though priests bemoan lower attendance at Mass, this remains a country where children are christened, marriages take place in churches, and crucifixes hang in public schools and government buildings. A secular parliament, whose members include Christian Democrats, the heirs of Mussolini's fascists, and communists, frequently listens to the Vatican's demands, and the pope and his bishops do not hesitate to attempt to influence elections and public referenda. When Italy's liberal assisted-fertility legislation was shot down in 2005, the Church might not have pulled the trigger but it certainly helped load the gun; newly elected Pope Benedict XVI led the charge a year later to defeat a referendum that would have restored the laws that made in vitro fertilization available to most Italian women.[3]

Walk down any street in Rome and you will find a Catholic church, a chapel, or at least an icon—an image of the Virgin Mary or of someone's patron saint—painted and revered on a corner wall.

Religion is not logical. It is based on faith, not reason. Religious faith involves beliefs that are not empirical and cannot be proven with mathematical formulas or scientific exactitude. They are beliefs that derive from another world, a metaphysical place beyond what we see, hear, and touch. In the last couple of centuries, however, Christian denominations in the West have sought to straddle the conflict between logic and religion by saying that the two do not have to be incompatible and can, with some effort, coexist. Especially after the reforms drafted and instituted in the Second Vatican Council, a historic, far-reaching policy consultation that the Church hierarchy underwent in the mid-1960s, the worshippers of the Catholic faith were told they could both think and believe. The mind, after all, was God's gift, and it should be used to its fullest God-given ability. Still, a determined segment of the Catholic Church passionately embraces beliefs that hark back to ancient times when the inexplicable was acceptable; for them it is a test of faith. In that religious context, belief in Satan, and in the power of prayer to combat him, is an easy-to-make leap of faith. As with all articles of faith, such belief requires the suspension of logic and reason, but as long as the believer is well-intentioned and guided by spiritually sound doctrine, he or she is on the right path.

Catholicism and other major religions have many beliefs at their core that fall into this category. Devout Catholics believe that there are obvious and undeniable truths that are beyond science, bigger than science, and that looking to logic will only lead to confusion. They are convinced, for example, that prayer can result in miraculous cures for the sick. In fact, for the Church to recognize and canonize a person as a saint, two miracles must be attributed to that person after his or her death. The Vatican uses a board of medical doctors, most of them Italian and all of them Catholic, to certify that the cure in question cannot be explained by science. The doctors examine the evidence at hand, evaluate the cure, and in many cases, judge it unexplainable by scientific knowledge of the day. With that medical stamp of approval, the Vatican declares the cure a miracle and the candidate is first beatified and later—after another miracle is documented—canonized. A saint is born, and the medical establishment has helped deliver it.

One of the most recent examples of this process

came in the beatification of Mother Teresa, the tiny eth-
nic Albanian Calcutta-based nun who became famous all
over the globe for her faith-based work with the poor and
sick. Teresa, who died in 1997 at the age of eighty-seven,
was beatified by Pope John Paul II in the autumn of 2003
after the "miraculous" cure of a Bengali tribal woman
was certified by the Vatican's board of medical consul-
tants. The woman, Monica Besra, was diagnosed with an
advanced ovarian tumor and sent in 1998 to die at an
Indian hospice run by Mother Teresa's Missionaries of
Charity. The nuns who attended Monica prayed to the
dead Mother Teresa for Monica's recovery. They placed
a medallion with Teresa's image on Monica's cancer-
ravaged abdomen. She recovered and the tumor disappeared.

Dr. Raffaello Cortesini, a heart-transplant specialist
who served as president of the Vatican's board of consul-
tants for two decades until retiring in 2002, sat on the
panel that validated Monica's cure. He said that in this
case, as in others he judged, the doctors on the board re-
viewed the medical evidence and eliminated the possibility of imaginary or hysterical phenomena. Under the
rules, the cure must be absolute, immediate, and without
scientific explanation. Cortesini, who recently worked a
stint at Columbia University in New York, said the board
concluded that Monica's cure could not be explained
medically. "This is divine intervention," he told me in
2003 when I interviewed him for the *Los Angeles Times*.
(Some doctors in Monica's hometown objected at the

time, saying she had received extensive medical treatment that could easily have shrunk the tumor. But the bandwagon for beatification of Mother Teresa was hard to stop.)[4]

The "miraculous" cure must occur after the would-be saint is dead because the cure has to come about when people pray to him or her. The cure then stands as proof that the would-be saint is with God, and that he or she can ask God to intercede on behalf of the sick person. Being with God is a prerequisite for becoming a saint.

In a sense, the recognition of miracles is like exorcism: These phenomena represent the intersection of ancient medieval thought and tradition with modern times. Science and rational thought are put aside, replaced by faith as its own form of spiritual truth.

Christian teaching holds that the devil, or Satan, was an angel who turned evil. God banished him to hell where he was joined by other rebelling bad angels who became demons. Thus evil is not contained in a single entity and there exist legions of malign spirits that dwell not in the physical realm but in a supernatural world. Because they don't have physical form, they must take possession of a victim's body and voice. Their goal, exorcists say, is to spread gratuitous hatred and challenge God.

Recognizing demonic possession—the "discernment," as it is called—is the first and very difficult aspect of an exorcism. This is most commonly achieved by seeing how the patient responds to religious symbols such as holy water or a crucifix. For example, the person has a great aversion to entering a church or cannot bear to face a priest. It must be said: Amorth and other exorcists insist that true demonic possession is extremely rare. In fact, of the thousands of Italians who seek exorcisms for themselves or for relatives, the priests say, few really need them. In most cases, the exorcist does not perform a full-fledged exorcism, but rather offers a prayer of "liberation," which includes some of the same incantations but does not involve the full ordeal.

Officially, the Catholic Church today is adamant about one thing: the need to establish that a person seeking an exorcism is not mentally or physically ill. This requirement is emphasized in the revised exorcism rite, which was formulated in 1999. Many exorcists say they work with psychiatrists and physicians to determine the nature of the patient's affliction. In a small number of cases, the doctors sign off on the patients, saying they've found no physical or mental illness to explain the patient's symptoms, and the exorcism is then authorized by a senior Church official, usually the bishop of the diocese where the patient lives or where he or she has sought help. However, in practice, exorcists disagree on the need for doctors to participate. Amorth usually asks the person seeking the exorcism whether he or she has first consulted a doctor (almost always they say they have) and he will take them at their word.

Like a number of the older exorcists, Amorth sees a diagnostic role for the exorcism itself. He maintains that the exorcism is the only procedure that can truly and definitively determine whether a person is afflicted by satanic influence. Only an exorcism, in his opinion, can overcome the tricks the devil uses to conceal his presence. The consequence of this is that some exorcisms take place without the consent of medical personnel. Since an exorcism is basically prayer, Amorth reasons, it can't hurt. "An unnecessary exorcism never harmed anyone," he says, rather controversially.

"It is only with the exorcism that one can arrive with certainty to the conclusion that the demon is present. Sometimes doctors can help. In the cases where there is doubt, where it is difficult to know if the illness is a product of evil or if the illness is something psychological, in these cases the presence of a psychiatrist is helpful. But that is very, very rare."

It is exactly that attitude that worries doctors, in Italy and elsewhere, who approach the subject of demonic possession and exorcism much more skeptically, or who think it is completely bogus. Ignoring physiological causes and medical advice risks exacerbating the patient's condition, they say. Furthermore, an exorcism can be highly suggestive, and a mentally unstable or otherwise susceptible patient could be convinced that he or she is possessed and could begin to display the symptoms out of imitation, compliance, or a subconscious need to please the priest.

"You promise something to someone who is very sick and at best you offer a temporary cure," says philosopher

Dr. Sergio Moravia of the University of Florence. "It's a scam."[5]

Amorth counters with the argument that people who come to him for exorcisms or healing prayers do so only after having recurring symptoms despite treatment from a host of doctors. If they had not exhausted medical possibilities, they would not be knocking on his door.

† † †

Priests divide the manifestation of demonic influence into several categories, the first few of which are considered more minor forms that can be helped with prayer and may not require an actual exorcism.

- Infestation of places, homes, businesses, animals, or objects. An exorcist can bless the place or object to rid it of evil spirits.
- Vexation. This is not possession but a kind of haunting of the victim. He or she is dogged by evil in the form of what appears to be a long spate of bad luck in work, love, or health.
- Obsession. The victim has uncontrollable evil thoughts that torment him or her, impeding the ability to enjoy life.
- Possession. This is the most serious, and most rare, form. An exorcism is the only recourse and can take years to cure the victim. Satan takes possession of the person and causes him or her to speak

and act without their knowledge or ability to control it. What distinguishes this condition from other forms of diabolical influence, as well as from purely worldly psychological disease, is that the victim reacts with visceral aversion to Christian symbols.

• Willful subjugation to the devil. This is really in a category by itself because the person has sought out the devil through satanic worship, black masses, which are rituals that mock and blaspheme Christian beliefs, or other overt activities. Such people almost never undergo exorcisms. Massimo Introvigne, Italy's leading expert on alternative religions and satanic cults, says that in twenty years of study, he has come across only one case of a Satanist who "converted" and sought deliverance from the devil through an exorcist.

The symptoms that often drive a person to seek an exorcist include a constant insurmountable malaise and physical pains that cannot be explained by medicine. The person has perhaps checked out medically; nothing is officially wrong with his or her body, stomach, head, or mind, and yet the person is tormented. While some Italian Catholics seem to seek out an exorcist almost like they would a hairdresser, many do so only as a last resort, after having sought help through many venues. With some exception, the possessed person might be able to sustain a relatively normal (if difficult) life until he or she confronts the exorcist. The "trance" brought on by the exorcism prayers is when the devil emerges and the more disturbing behavior manifests itself.

Amorth maintains that Catholics fall prey to the devil in four central ways. Sometimes it is God's work, a test or trial meant to increase the victim's humility. Other cases, especially in superstitious Italy, are the result of an evil spell cast by a mortal enemy with evil in his heart. (The Church frowns upon folkloric belief in spells and the "evil eye," but that does not stop a widespread following of such superstitions, especially in rural Italy.) The final two categories are the fastest growing: the victim lives in a "grave and hardened" state of sin, such as living with a partner without being married or having undergone an abortion; and the association with evil people or places, such as consulting with fortune-tellers, witches, or séance-conducting mediums. This final category is not the same as satanic worship but rather describes someone who dabbles a bit in the occult and thus becomes vulnerable to satanic possession.

"There has been a real boom in occult practices, and these customs are opening the door to evil spirits and to possessions themselves," Amorth said.

Dressed in a long black cloak, the balding, oval-faced Amorth is a serious but not frightening figure. As I observed the first time I met him, he's more Uncle Fester than Max von Sydow. His eyes are intense and piercing, encircled by dark rings. Yet his features also relax easily into a smile and chuckle. In later meetings with him, he seemed tired and spoke more slowly. He was sometimes forgetful and had lost some of his zip—but not the sparkle in his eyes.

Father Amorth was born in Modena, in northern Italy, and became a priest in 1954. In 1986, he started performing exorcisms under the tutelage of Cardinal Ugo Poletti, the vicar for Rome who died in 1997, and Father Candido Amantini, a renowned exorcist who died in 1992. Amorth said he accepted the task after praying to the Virgin Mary for her steadfast guidance and protection. Holy man to some, huckster to others, Amorth has written more than a dozen books on the topic of exorcism and is a dedicated champion of the need for more priests who can perform the ritual.

At the compound where Amorth and fellow priests of the Society of Saint Paul live and have their offices, Amorth receives his troubled flock and performs exorcisms, always in a room far removed from the street so no one hears the screams. "Otherwise, the police will come," Amorth said, with the faintest hint of a smile.

The walls are painted sea green, worn with cracked patches in the plaster. In all, the room is about six feet by nine, has five or six straight-backed chairs pushed up against the walls, and has one slightly more padded vinyl chair where Amorth said patients who are not in very critical condition can sit. The helpers sit in the other chairs and can include other priests, family members of the patient, or assistants to control the patient. Amorth also often uses several pious lay members of the Charismatic Renewal movement to help with the prayers. "You need much prayer," he says. The patients who are more volatile or more sick lie on a blue padded bed, like one from a doctor's office, and may be strapped in. Amorth showed me the coil of inch-wide binding straps he uses. Violence is always a possibility; hence the need for helpers. Few priests will conduct an exorcism alone.

On the walls of Amorth's exorcism chamber, eight crucifixes and pictures of the Madonna are hanging, plus a picture of Saint Michael the Archangel. A two-foot-high statue of the Virgin Mary, the Madonna of Fatima, sits on a corner table. There are also pictures of the late Pope John Paul II; the popular Italian saint Padre Pio; Amorth's mentor, Father Candido; and Father Giacomo Alberione, the founder of the Society of Saint Paul congregation. "My protectors," Amorth calls them, adding that the more recent addition of John Paul's picture has been especially effective and helpful. "The demons become very agitated at his presence."

At the very top of one wall there is a small window, curtains drawn, and an air conditioner.

Amorth keeps the tools of his trade ever at his side, sheathed in a weathered leather bag: a silver and wooden crucifix, a silver aspergillum for the sprinkling of holy water, and a vial of consecrated oil. In addition, he uses a purple priest's stole and the hardcover prayer book with the approved exorcism intonations.

Technically speaking, even a baptism is a form of exorcism, as are daily prayers of liberation and other religious rituals of cleansing. In the case of babies who are baptized, for example, the baptism cleanses the child of original sin and allows it to enter heaven should it die; otherwise, the baby, though an innocent, languishes in limbo, a state short of hell but not in heaven. (The Church is reviewing its teachings on limbo, and some of these rather unforgiving judgments may be changed.) Amorth says he often prefers to use the term "blessing" instead of "exorcism" so as not to unduly alarm the patient.

The Catholic Catechism, the prime set of guidelines that instructs every Catholic on how to be a good one, states: "When the Church asks publicly and with authority, in the name of Jesus Christ, that a person or an object be protected against the power of the Evil One and withdrawn from his dominion, it is called exorcism."[6] That kind of exorcism can be nothing more than a series of prayers for a patient who is "vexed" or disturbed, but not possessed. These are usually short and uneventful rituals. It is in the realm of the "major exorcism," however, that the more dramatic and violent events take place. A major exorcism is what Father Efrem and Caterina the dancer were involved in. It is administered only for the cases that Church officials have determined are authentic demonic possessions. Of the scores of people who seek comfort from Father Amorth, he told me, only a tiny fraction of them are truly possessed and in need of a full-blown exorcism. That same trend is repeated across the country:

even among those faithful who readily believe in the existence of Satan and his ability to control people, the consensus is that true diabolical possession is rare.

When it is deemed real, however, the Catechism, which has been updated periodically to reflect the times, is explicit in its handling of the "major exorcisms":

> The priest must proceed with prudence, rigorously observing the rules established by the Church. The exorcism is directed at the expulsion of demons or to the liberation from demonic possession, through the spiritual authority that Jesus has entrusted to his Church. Very different is the case of illness, especially psychological illness, whose treatment belongs to the field of medical science. It is important, therefore, to ascertain, before performing an exorcism, that what is involved is the presence of the Evil One and not a sickness.[7]

And so, as noted earlier, exorcists are supposed to consult with doctors before proceeding, and in many Italian dioceses, a team of doctors and psychiatrists has been established to work with the Church on precisely these kinds of cases. Yet it is clear, countrywide, that this rule is not always followed rigorously.

"In the majority of cases, the people who come to me are not in need of an exorcism but of medical care. But when some people, after having gone through extensive medical treatment, have had no benefits, they begin to think their problems are not natural," Amorth said. "And the reality is, medicine is limited and often incapable of supplying diagnoses and cures. Especially with many forms of schizophrenia, medicine still has a long way to go. And sometimes a person thinks he's possessed and resorts to the exorcist but then finds there's no evil spirit. It's sad."

An exorcism begins with prayer. The exorcist places the purple stole over the patient and makes the sign of the cross. The patient is supposed to say the prayers in unison with the priest, who may also anoint the patient with the oil and holy water. A truly possessed person experiences uncontrollable aversion to the sacraments, to all things holy and sacred. Thus can begin the physical convulsions, the fury-filled bellicose reactions, and the voices—a deep booming voice cursing the priest; a small, effeminate voice pleading for help.

There are four consistent symptoms of true possession, exorcists say, and this checklist has remained largely unchanged since medieval times:

- manifestation of superhuman strength
- the speaking in tongues or in languages that the victim cannot know
- the revelation of knowledge, distant or hidden, that the victim cannot know
- blasphemic rage and an aversion to holy symbols

Father Amorth and other exorcists claim that in the most extreme cases, they have seen these signs and even more; in the case of Caterina, we heard the voices and saw the rage. The devil, Amorth says, is fighting the intervention of the priest, resisting the expulsion, and will pull out all the stops to thwart God's work. In some exorcisms, patients have revealed the secrets hidden by the priest or one of the attendants. "They can talk about the sins of the exorcist, to try to demoralize him," Amorth said. "But I always say that I, too, am protected. I turned to the Madonna and asked that she protect me, and she has always come through. I've never been afraid of the devil. In fact, I can say," he added with satisfaction, "the devil is afraid of me."

The exorcist must attempt to interrogate the demon, Amorth explains. He will command the demon to state his name, but the evil spirit often has a hard time doing so. The exorcist asks a series of questions that are "useful for the liberation" and never out of simple curiosity: State your name. When did you enter this person? Under what circumstances? When will you leave, by order of Jesus Christ?

The exorcism crescendos with the priest ordering Satan to be gone. Rarely, if ever, are patients cured in a single session. Some of Amorth's patients have been with him for years; the record holder, sixteen years. "Even if they are not cured, they receive advantages, so as to lead a normal life," Amorth said. "Not always with exorcism can you liberate a person, but you can always give relief."

While it is highly unusual for outsiders to attend an exorcism, Amorth is more than willing to display a small collection of items he says patients have "vomited." He believes they don't actually vomit these items from their stomachs, as there is never any physical damage to the throat or esophagus. Rather, the items appear in the mouth of the person as he or she gags and chokes. He exhibited several AA Duracell batteries, a small chain, numerous screws about two inches long, and a small man-from-outer-space toy. He keeps the items in a clutch of old, torn envelopes, stuffed inside a larger envelope.

These are the kinds of stories that outsiders find especially hard to believe, and Amorth acknowledges that much of what he says invites skepticism. Even within his own church hierarchy there is some resistance; some exorcists say they have not witnessed these more bizarre feats. And it doesn't help that Amorth sees the devil in many places: a couple of years ago he fought to ban publication in Italy of the Harry Potter books because, he said, they teach sorcery to children. He argues that the growth of evil in the world constitutes overwhelming proof that Satan is working overtime. One need look no further than ritualistic murders, satanic cults that torture and rape victims, a spate of horrific child abuse cases, and so forth. A society bereft of values and moral codes has created a fertile field for evil. Who could deny it? In fact, the devil's most clever trick is to make people doubt his existence.

"I know there is a lot of skepticism," Amorth said. "A

lot of damage is done by priests specialized in the holy scriptures who deny exorcisms, even those performed by Jesus Christ. The presence of the demon is often ignored."

According to Amorth, a good exorcist is a priest who is especially devout and who is purged of sin. He must be clean, because otherwise the devil can take advantage of his weakness. It is particularly helpful if the priest has a special devotion to the Virgin Mary, because she is a notably fierce enemy of Satan. In a practical sense, the exorcist must be a man of steel nerves and endless patience who is not thrown for a loop when strange things happen before his eyes.

The Roman Ritual (Rituale Romanum), which contains the formal rules for an exorcism, sets out these guidelines:[8]

- In every case, the exorcist has to evaluate with appropriate attention whether the possession is real or a figment of the person's imagination. Each case must be examined with the greatest caution to determine whether the person is possessed or suffering from disease, especially of a psychic nature.
- The priest who becomes an exorcist must be of proven devotion, knowledge, prudence, and integrity; and must pray and fast to obtain God's help.
- The exorcism must be carried out in such a way as to manifest the faith of the Church and to prevent

the rite from being interpreted as an act of magic or superstition.

- The tormented one should, as much as is possible, prepare for the exorcism with prayer, communion, confession, and fasting.
- The exorcism should be conducted in an oratory, a chapel, or small room for devotional prayers in a church, if possible, avoiding the presence of many people. The image of the crucifix must be dominant, as well as an image of the Virgin Mary. Parents, friends, the confessor, or the spiritual director of the person undergoing the exorcism can be present to help the exorcist in the prayers, especially if he can derive strength from their charity and proximity.
- The rite begins with the aspersion of holy water, and the exorcist must show the tormented one the Lord's cross. If necessary, the rite can be repeated, either immediately or at another time, until the tormented one is completely free.
- The exorcist should be vested in cassock, surplice, and a violet stole.

By some estimates offered by Italian mental health organizations, thousands of Italians seek exorcisms every year. Amorth is reluctant to pinpoint a number, and he contends that, regrettably, many more people frequent practitioners of witchcraft and black magic. Whatever the number, there is no doubt that demand has soared.

As Amorth put it in one of his essays:

> Why, today, is there such a high demand for
> exorcists? Can we make the case that the
> demon is more active today than in the past?
> Can we say that the incidence of demonic
> possession and other, lesser, evil disturbances
> is on the rise? The answer to these and simi-
> lar questions is a decisive Yes. Rationalism,
> Atheism—which is preached to the masses—
> and the corruption that is a by-product of
> Western consumerism have all contributed to
> a frightening decline in faith.
>
> This I can state with mathematical cer-
> tainty: where faith declines, superstition
> grows.[9]

CHAPTER III

History

That evening they brought to [Jesus] many
who were oppressed by demons, and he cast
out the spirits with a word and healed all who
were sick.

—Matthew 8:16,
Revised Standard Version

And immediately there was in their syna-
gogue a man with an unclean spirit. And he
cried out, "What have you to do with us,
Jesus of Nazareth? Have you come to destroy
us? I know who you are—the Holy One of
God." But Jesus rebuked him, saying, "Be
silent, and come out of him!" And the unclean

31

spirit, convulsing him and crying out with a
loud voice, came out of him.

—Mark 1:23–26, RSV

And he healed many who were sick with various diseases, and cast out many demons.
And he would not permit the demons to
speak, because they knew him. . . . And he
went throughout all Galilee, preaching in
their synagogues and casting out demons.

—Mark 1:34, 39, RSV

Again, the devil took him to a very high
mountain and showed him all the kingdoms
of the world and their glory. And he said to
him, "All these I will give you, if you will fall
down and worship me." Then Jesus said to
him, "Be gone, Satan! For it is written, 'You
shall worship the Lord your God and him
only shall you serve.'" Then the devil left him,
and behold, angels came and were ministering
to him.

—Matthew 4:8–11, RSV

Ancient cultures from as long ago as the Babylonians
and the Egyptian pharaohs speak of demonic entities and
forms of exorcism. The word *demon* comes from the clas-
sical Greek *daimon* or *daimonion*, which means "to be

mad." The word *satan* comes from the Hebrew for "adversary" or "opponent," and the word *devil* from Old English *deofel*, Latin *diabolus*, and Greek *diabolos*. Other names used in Christianity include Lucifer, Beelzebub, Zebulun, Meridian, and Belial.[1] In other words, there has been no shortage of monikers throughout the ages and the cultures to give recognition to a central embodied force of evil.

The devil appears in the Bible and with frequency in the New Testament, where he tempts Jesus in the desert. He appears century after century in art and literature, from Dante's *Inferno* to cartoon depictions of him as a man with horns and a pitchfork. In one Italian cinematic version, he is portrayed as a Mafioso dressed in Armani.

Jesus was Christianity's first major exorcist. He was a healer, and physical and mental illnesses of the day, such as blindness, the inability to speak, madness, and so forth, were often attributed to evil spirits. By casting out the demons, Jesus was able to heal the sick and afflicted, which also added weight to the arguments of the time that he was the messiah, the Chosen One empowered to do, and doing, God's work on earth. Jesus also empowered his disciples and apostles to cast out demons in his name.

Judaism, Islam, and other religions contain elements of exorcism, cleansing rituals, or "deliverance," as Protestants call it. But only the Roman Catholic Church has so thoroughly codified and institutionalized the practice.

Pope Cornelius in the third century wrote of the existence of fifty-two exorcists in the Roman Catholic Church.[2] For many centuries, a separate office of exorcism existed in the Church, but as Christianity spread through the Western world, it was phased out, and instead, all priests upon ordination were granted the authority to conduct exorcisms. (This, too, would later change.) Belief in the devil has ebbed and flowed through history, but it grew steadily during the Middle Ages, when people readily blamed problems, natural disasters, disease, and any number of contretemps on swarming hordes of demons, as noted by historian Jeffrey Burton Russell, who has written extensively on the devil.[3] It was also a tumultuous time for the Church, plagued with corruption and fighting a revolution from reform-minded progressives who would eventually break away to form the Protestant church. For some conservative Church forces, it may have been useful to sustain fear of Satan.

Evil is not a concept, it is not abstract, for many people. It is a thing, a powerful, pulsating, living thing that makes people do wrong. Satan, as the chief doer of evil, comes from God's teachings in the Bible. Besides, how else are some events explained? A love is lost because a rival used the power of evil to cast a spell; a war springs up for no reason; a vast plague . . . these are proof of the devil's work.

But can we believe that? Exorcists do. They expel the devil. For them, Catholic Church doctrine is clear on the subject: the devil is real, not a reflection of evil in mankind.

Christianity flows from Judaism. In the earliest days, those we now call Christians saw themselves as a true-believing branch of Judaism following a rabbi called Jesus. And there are many students of the Bible who see the devil as an evil force clearly present in the Hebrew Bible, the Old Testament. Others can't find him there and say that the devil first comes to life in Christian writing in the final book of the New Testament (Revelation) and was only developed into something now familiar during the following centuries of Christianity.

Translating ancient texts can produce debate over the proper words to choose and the contemporary meaning of the ideas in question, especially when there were several original languages, some barely spoken for centuries. The fact that today there are so many rival versions of the Bible in English alone—each certain that it's the correct one—might make them all suspect. According to some scholars, common translations of the word *satan* in the Old Testament describe someone who is only an adversary, an accuser, or someone who is an obstacle. He is not supreme in evil, or in anything else; rather, Satan is shown as a sort of bureaucrat in God's divine council, under God's supervision. He torments Job, for instance, but he does so to test Job's piety toward God.[4]

No one disputes that the Old Testament certainly has stories of a struggle between good and evil—Adam and Eve lost in that struggle and so did their son Cain; their other son Abel lost his life—but some believe that evil was more a concept than a leering creature with horns and a pitchfork. They claim that the Hebrew Bible does not say that the serpent who lured Eve represented the thing called "the devil." The more sinister interpretations they find much later.

In the New Testament Satan becomes something a bit more recognizable to us today. He does evil things. He strengthens Jesus's earthly enemies. For example, Judas's betrayal is at the prompting of the devil. He changes from a member of God's entourage to someone who opposes God. The devil has become bold enough to tempt Jesus in the wilderness. Jesus is seen to be in a fight with evil, which, for some scholars, takes the form of Satan. In this fight, Jesus is said to have the power to cure the sick by casting out demons—what could be called exorcism—and he shares this with his apostles, which becomes the basis for priests having the power to do the same. Though in the context of those ancient times many people who were simply sick or infirm could have been taken to be the victims of what was called a *demon*.

It is toward the end of the book of Revelation that the devil finally has an army of demons and a body. What a terrifying body! "A great red dragon, with seven heads and ten horns, and on his heads seven diadems. His tail swept down a third of the stars of heaven and cast them to the earth" (Rev. 12:3–4, RSV). Up to the fight swings the angel Michael, with his own army, and he defeats Satan and his demons. But, some believe, the devil and his demons are what must be defeated again in exorcisms.

That the devil lived—perhaps just down the road—

36

was a certainty in the minds of many Christians for many centuries. The idea was not only Church teaching; it was fed by and reinforced unsophisticated people's fear of a world where the most awful things were unfathomable, like a village suddenly destroyed by disease, or those unseen forces that could make the clouds go gray and then make water fall in drops, or five years of murderous famine. Of course it was the devil who caused these things. And if the priest, through his special relationship with God, might relieve the oppression, people might turn to the priest, which also pulled them closer to the Church and made it more important.

But by the early 1500s the Catholic Church that made people feel at least somewhat protected against the unpredictable and unexplainable was itself under a quiet but very strong, debilitating attack. In 1517 Martin Luther began the assault. By mid-century Protestantism was unrolling across much of Europe. The Vatican had lost England and was forced to sign a treaty to allow Lutherans to share Germany with Catholics. To Catholics, all of this was undeniably more than a political offense, it was heresy. Clearly, without doubt, it was caused by the forces of evil. The devil was at work.

Still, for some fifteen centuries after Jesus, exorcism was not as common as it would become. Exorcism grew just at the time when the Church—and its faithful—saw a mortal danger to tradition, accepted hierarchy, and a system whereby the Church kept things the way they were supposed to be. Interestingly, this coincided with the beginnings of better explanations for what people feared.

While some in Europe were finding that the developing scientific theories could answer some questions and were trying to nestle scientific findings alongside Christian doctrine, there were many others who saw that the essential religious as well as the secular truths of centuries were being diminished. The Church was losing its monopoly on truth, and with that, it was losing control over what held society together. The threat was even worse in Italy, where the Vatican controlled the secular world as well as the religious.

It may be more than random coincidence that in northern Italy two renowned men were deeply involved in this controversy, and were pulling in opposite directions at around the same time.

The early European scientist Galileo Galilei, born in Pisa in 1564, ran against the deeply accepted notion that wisdom came from absorbing what earlier thinkers had taught and especially from current Catholic interpretations of the Bible. Instead, Galileo said it was also necessary to use observation and experimentation to understand the nature of things. His initial work seems so rudimentary now, but his unorthodox approach eventually became part of the basics of scientific inquiry. Still, while he was alive, the Church felt so undermined by his research that it put him in a dungeon and threatened much worse.

After watching a suspended lamp swing in the cathedral of Pisa, Galileo experimented with the uses of the pendulum to tell time. He went against Aristotle's teachings and used the tower at Pisa to show that objects of different weights fall with the same speed. He made a telescope and found a universe much more complex than the Church taught. He even said science proved that the earth revolved around the sun. The Church said holy scripture taught the exact opposite, and sent in the Inquisition to change Galileo's mind.

The Church asserted that faith was more powerful than science. After all, faith was believing in that which could not be proven. The belief that the earth was the center of the universe, like the belief in demons, had begun in antiquity and been absorbed into Christian doctrine. It was one of those ideas that was undeniably true because it had always been true.

The other man, Father Girolamo Menghi, was born in 1529 in Viadana, eighty miles from Galileo's Pisa. He studied as a theologian and became a famous researcher like Galileo. But Menghi's work was pulling together writings on the devil and on exorcism, because the body of beliefs had changed spectacularly since the Bible. Man had updated the gospel.[5]

Some early Christian scholars wrote that the devil lived in the air, keeping a watch on his victims. Saint Augustine taught that demons were made of air. Demons had specialized duties, the bishop of Marseille preached in the fifth century; some performed cruel acts, or lascivious ones, some tempted humans, and others played pranks. Saint Thomas Aquinas wrote that one of the main duties of demons was to torture the sinners in hell's fires. In Constantinople, another leading scholar said that, in fact, demons entered humans and animals to get warm.

By the 1300s, through *The Divine Comedy*, Dante's imagination had given believers a detailed, precise image of hell, a notion to hold in their minds during moments of temptation: Hell had nine circles funneling into the earth, and sinners were cast down to the circle that fit their sins. In the center of the lowest ring sat Satan, eating the worst of the damned.

Father Menghi seems to have been the first scholar to specialize in the problems that warranted exorcism. He took the hundreds of post-biblical teachings on the devil and demons—sometimes contradictory theories—and added his own ideas. He preached that there were many types of demons, in a hierarchy of rank and responsibility reminiscent of the Greek and Roman gods, that existed from the time not long before and not long after the birth of Jesus. There were demons who lived almost beyond the sky. He called these the "fiery ones." There were others living closer to earth who, Menghi said, were haughty and drove victims to be conceited. The demons on the earth, the Terreo, enticed their victims with worldly and base temptations. Others skulked in seas and lakes to sink ships. Others lived underground, collaborating with magicians and sorcerers, and still others were afraid of light. All of them were crafty and worked with the devil's ability to see the future.

Witches, he said, had sex with demons, learned sorcery, and made pacts with them over controlling people.

All of this may seem to be a wild amalgam of ancient beliefs, folk stories, fairy tales of wicked elves, black magic, and fanciful interpretations of the Bible. But the Church did not seem to take it that way.

Menghi listed the signs of a person who is possessed by demons, or the devil.

They are:

- the ability to speak languages previously unknown to them
- revealing facts they could not have known
- superhuman strength
- the sudden, sometimes violent, aversion to priests and sacraments
- deep melancholy
- calling for the devil's help
- vomiting of bizarre objects, like knives or pieces of glass

It is virtually the same checklist that Catholic exorcists go by today.

In 1576 Father Menghi published an extended handbook for exorcists. It described each step they must take, the wording of prayers, when to make the sign of the cross, when the priest should put his stole on the victim, and so on. The Church then issued its own manual for exorcists with many of the same instructions, which are very similar to its current guidelines. Father Menghi's work was endorsed by the Vatican.

It went much differently for Galileo: he was brought before the Inquisition. Pope Urban VIII, a longtime personal friend, arrested the scientist and threw him in a dungeon. Facing the pope's threats of extreme torture, a now-elderly Galileo gave in. He swore that he had been wrong to say that the earth revolved around the sun, and he begged to be allowed to live. It turned out that faith really was more powerful than science.

† † †

Between the fourteenth and seventeenth centuries, belief in Satan's power reached manic levels, which in turn fueled the witch craze. Tens of thousands of people, primarily women, were burned at the stake or otherwise punished for supposedly practicing witchcraft, casting spells, or other demonic deeds. Eventually the Church saw a need to crack down. As a result, by the eighteenth century the exorcism rite began to fall out of favor. In addition, a historical period of scientific and medical advances, and eventually development of the field of psychology, pushed thinking in other directions, even within the Church. Philosophical trends such as the Enlightenment and Rationalism gave precedence to reason over emotion, the laws of nature over ritualistic tra-

42

dition and superstition. The Church slowly came to terms with the modern age, and for much of the nineteenth- and twentieth-century Church hierarchy, exorcism became an embarrassing, unsavory ancient ritual that was best forgotten.

Today a number of theologians argue that Satan does not exist, at least not in the concrete way that exorcists envision.

Exorcism was not without its champions during this period. In 1879, Father Francisco Palau, a Carmelite from Spain who is said to have devoted his life to healing the demonically possessed, traveled to Rome to implore the Vatican to reestablish the office of exorcist as a permanent, separate ministry of the church. He failed.[6] The pontiff at the time, Pope Leo XIII, who reigned from 1878 until his death in 1903, is credited with authorship of a prayer that, for about a century, was recited by congregations on their knees at the end of many a Mass: "St. Michael the Archangel, defend us in battle, be our protector against the wickedness and snares of the devil; may God rebuke him, we humbly pray; and do thou, O Prince of the heavenly host, by the power of God, thrust into hell Satan and all the evil spirits who wander through the world for the ruin of souls. Amen."

Father Amorth and others say Pope Leo XIII wrote and instituted this prayer after experiencing a vision of demonic spirits who were attempting to converge on Rome. In addition, the pope, who was known for recognizing contemporary trends without compromising his deeply conservative piety, wrote an exorcism prayer that was included in the Roman Ritual.

The ebb and flow of exorcism also reflects a wider struggle within the Church on how to regard Satan, how to strike the balance between becoming overly preoccupied with him and ignoring him. At least by the twentieth century, the Church discouraged excessive credulity and an obsession with demons that might lead to superstition rather than well-grounded theological interpretation. At the same time, Church leaders rejected an exclusive reliance on the rationalist's approach that would deny the possibility of diabolical infections and chalk up every phenomenon to medical science.

Today the Church is cautious about giving a definitive description of the devil and prefers to cast distinctions between personal and impersonal evil in more abstract terms, notes Church historian Father Norman Tanner at Rome's Pontifical Gregorian University. "Christ firmly believed in the reality of evil and a personal devil. He does not go into details. It is an invisible world, like for angels, an other-worldly realm," Tanner, a Jesuit, said. "The Catholic Church has always insisted on the ultimate freedom to choose God and the possibility to overcome evil. Obviously, it must be done with God's grace."[7]

The tension over exorcism also springs in part from the Church's fundamental belief that the devil is an entity that is inferior to God. According to the Bible, Satan was an angel created by God who rebelled; thus the battle is always an imbalanced one that God will always ulti-mately win. Satan is the insurgent commander to God as the king. The two should never be seen as equals or in a parallel duality.

The Catechism puts it this way:

> The power of Satan is, nonetheless, not infi-nite. He is only a creature, powerful from the fact that he is pure spirit, but still a creature. He cannot prevent the building up of God's reign. Although Satan may act in the world out of hatred for God and his kingdom in Christ Jesus, and although his action may cause grave injuries—of a spiritual nature and, indirectly, even of a physical nature—to each man and to society, the action is permit-ted by divine providence which with strength and gentleness guides human and cosmic his-tory. It is a great mystery that providence should permit diabolical activity, but "we know that in everything God works for good with those who love him" (Romans 8:28).[8]

Indeed, one of the most persistent questions in moral theology is why God permits evil. If there is a God, a stu-dent might ask, then why was there the Holocaust or the tsunami that killed tens of thousands of people? How can he allow such dastardly events to happen?

By the time the Second Vatican Council rolled

around in the mid-1960s, exorcism was, as Amorth put it, a neglected sacrament. The spirit of modernization possessed the 1962–1965 Vatican II, and Church leaders frowned upon clearly medieval, controversial, and in the view of many, backward rites such as exorcism. In the drafting of the Second Vatican Council guidelines, emphasis was placed on good, hope, and compassion, and discussion of evil and demons was minimized. As a result of Vatican II, a host of Church documents were updated and revised, but the Roman Ritual governing exorcism was shoved to a back burner. And instead of conferring on all priests upon ordination the duty to serve as an exorcist, the Church declared that only bishops could appoint exorcists and authorize exorcisms.

Then the pendulum began to swing the other way. Pope Paul VI, who oversaw the last half of Vatican II, became alarmed at theological negation of the existence of the devil and his work. He felt the need to set the record straight at a general audience in 1972:

> Evil is not merely a lack of something, but an effective agent, a living spiritual being, perverted and perverting. A terrible reality. Mysterious and frightening. It is contrary to the teaching of the Bible and the Church to refuse to recognize the existence of such a reality, or to regard it as a principle in itself which does not draw its origin from God like every other creature; or to explain it as a

pseudo-reality, a conceptual and fanciful personification of the unknown cause of our
misfortunes.[9]

Meanwhile, in the popular culture interest in exorcism was returning, in part as a reaction to a perceived
proliferation of black magic and satanic cults. Exorcism's
comeback was also fueled by the steady growth in the
1970s and 1980s of the Catholic Charismatic Renewal
movement, a Pentecostal faction that believes in healing
and prophecy. On top of this, exorcism was clearly
viewed favorably by Pope John Paul II, who frequently referred to Satan as a real and present dangerous force in
the world. And, it must be said, the success of the movie
The Exorcist also helped stir up interest, especially in the
United States.

In 1987, John Paul visited the Sanctuary of Saint
Michael the Archangel and said: "The battle against the
devil . . . is still being fought today, because the devil is
still alive and active in the world. The evil that surrounds
us today, the disorders that plague our society, man's in-
consistency and brokenness, are not only the results of
original sin, but also the result of Satan's pervasive and
dark action."

John Paul, whose faith was mystical, visceral, and
emotional, devoted hours upon hours of prayer and reverence to Mary, enemy of Satan. He is reported to have
performed at least three exorcisms.

The first one, according to veteran Vatican journalist

Sandro Magister, occurred in 1978 when Father Candido Amantini, the famous exorcist based at Rome's Santa Scala Church and Father Amorth's mentor, asked the pope for assistance. Few details are known.

John Paul performed another exorcism at the Vatican in March 1982 on a young woman identified only as Francesca F., according to the late cardinal Jacques-Paul Martin, prefect of the papal household. Martin recounted the incident in his memoirs, as cited by the Italian news agency Ansa. A bishop brought Francesca F. before the pope. Upon seeing him, she screamed and convulsed on the floor. According to Martin, she only returned to normal when the pope said, "Tomorrow I will say Mass for you." Magister adds that Francesca F. returned a year later to visit the pope, in the company of her husband, and was calm, happy, and expecting a child.[10]

A third exorcism is believed to have been performed in 2000 and involved a nineteen-year-old woman from the Italian town of Monza who arrived for the pope's weekly public audience at Saint Peter's Square, where he would routinely deliver a message to the thousands of people who gathered to see him. The young woman was hunchbacked and moved with difficulty, so organizers placed her in a front row reserved for people with physical disabilities. But when the pope appeared, she burst into shouts, spewed vulgarities, and writhed violently. Guards wanted to remove her, but the pope asked that she be taken to one side so that he could bless her. At the conclusion of the audience, after a turn through the square on his pope-mobile, John Paul spent about a half hour praying with the woman in a private room just inside the Vatican walls. He promised to say a Mass for her. But he failed to rid her of the demon, according to Amorth, who recalled the episode and also examined the woman. Amorth says that the next day, the woman said to him in a deep, booming voice, "Not even the pope was able to defeat me."

The core script of the exorcism rite was written in 1614 and remained virtually unchanged for 385 years. Only in 1999 was a new document (ninety pages in its Latin version) issued by the Vatican, the first significant revision of the rite: "De Exorcismus et Supplicationibus Quibusdam" (Concerning Exorcisms and Certain Supplications). It was the last of the Church's major documents to be revised after Vatican II, its delay a reflection of both how delicate a subject it was and how unimportant it was to some segments of the Church that were more concerned with reforms with wider impact, such as how Sunday Mass would be conducted. In the new exorcism rite, most prayers and exhortations were not altered, but the document included a new warning against confusing psychiatric illness with possession and urged priests to use "maximum circumspection and prudence" in deciding to exorcise. It formalized the requirement that an exorcist be appointed by a bishop, or short of that, specific exorcisms should be authorized individually by a bishop.

Cardinal Jorge Arturo Medina Estevez, a Chilean,

presided at the time over the Congregation for Divine
Worship, which was in charge of the revisions. He said it
took ten years of consultation, study, and debated modi-
fications to come up with the new document, even
though changes were minimal. A committee of cardinals
from Rome and bishops from outlying constituencies
participated. Most of the changes, he said, had to do with
toning down some of the more gruesome medieval language used to describe the devil. And while the older version includes a line whereby the exorcist commands the
devil to leave the possessed person, the new version calls
on God to command the devil to leave. (The new version,
placed in Vatican bookstores, sold "like hotcakes," a senior Church official said.)

As with all its documents, the Vatican issued the new
book of rituals in Latin, and bishops' conferences in various countries were then expected to translate it into
their local language. Medina said the first languages of
translation were Portuguese, Polish, and Italian.[11]

An especially conservative cardinal, Medina has precise ideas about possession and the devil. "The possessed
person is not sinning, because to sin, you need to act with
your free will," Medina said. "The possessed person is en-
slaved by the devil.

"But the devil is very smart. Usually he does not act
through possession; rather, he acts through temptation.
And since the demon is a liar he is able to tempt by making bad things look good. He tricks people into thinking
they can find happiness in ways that act against the law of

God. For example, he makes people think they don't have to obey the laws of fidelity in marriage because they can resolve the situation through divorce. Or he makes people believe abortion is okay because he convinces them that the conceived creature is not a human being but just a bunch of cells that can be thrown away the way someone has a cough and spits."[12]

According to Medina, the Church maintains that such temptation can be overcome through prayer, the catechism, and education; exorcism is not necessary. Nor should exorcism be applied in cases in which a person thinks he or she has been cursed with the evil eye a common occurrence in Italy. Those people need spiritual guidance, the Church says, not an exorcism.

A few months after the new rite was released, the Church issued separate guidelines aimed at clamping down on unauthorized exorcisms and mass faith-healing ceremonies. There was speculation at the time that the orders were directed at Emmanuel Milingo, who was crisscrossing Italy to hold revival-style meetings that included public exorcisms and "healings," all in a manner not appreciated by the Roman Catholic Church. Whether or not his activities prompted the document, its authors stated clearly that they were responding to the "proliferation of prayer meetings" that included healing and were part of the burgeoning Charismatic movement.

The document dictated ten disciplinary norms that recognized the importance of prayer to God for healing but said such supplications had to follow established rules and come under the guidance of the diocesan bishop. "Anything resembling hysteria, artificiality, theatricality, or sensationalism, above all on the part of those who are in charge of such gatherings, must not take place," the instructions stated. Neither healing prayers nor exorcisms should ever be included in the Holy Mass so as not to confuse expectations raised by the former with the sanctity of the latter.

These new restrictions were issued by the Congregation for the Doctrine of the Faith, the main Church body that oversees dogma, and signed by its then-prefect, Cardinal Joseph Ratzinger.

Taken together, these two documents addressed complementary concerns. The Church was tacitly acknowledging that exorcisms were again popular and in demand; that said, Church leaders wanted to attempt to keep abuse in check. Begrudged acceptance, yes, while maintaining control and ensuring a measure of decorum. Undoubtedly this is a problem for the Church—the Bible, Jesus, and the pope all endorse exorcism, yet it is an easily abused archaic ritual that could all too readily be used to make the Church look bad and discourage thoughtful obedience to other, more mainstream aspects of Catholicism.

Father Amorth and some of the more traditional exorcists still use the old rite and shrug off the changes contained in the new. But they feel vindicated that growing acceptance of the practice has reached the highest echelons of today's Vatican.

In fact, the Church's official view today is nuanced and reflects a certain ambivalence, as is so often the case with pronouncements from the Holy See. Officially, the Church leadership approves of the use of exorcisms, but at the same time it does not want the ritual to become common, a subject of mass hysteria, or exaggerated. Church leaders clearly fear abuse of the rite. Rather than a matter of hot debate within the Church, however, exorcism and the idea of demonic possession seem to be topics that many priests simply prefer to push to the periphery. Yet even the most liberal priest cannot dismiss the notion of evil and the healing power of prayer; these are concepts that are central to Church teaching. What priests do disagree on is the extent to which evil is personified in a "real" entity like Satan.

At one end of the spectrum is Cardinal Tarcisio Bertone, until recently the archbishop of Genoa. "The devil is real, he is at work, and he is agitating," he told me in 2004. "We must fight him." I interviewed Bertone in Genoa at his regal church, Santa Maria Auxiliatrice, shortly after he announced the appointment of a task force of exorcists and physicians to collaborate in weeding out people with mental disturbances from those in need of exorcisms. The reason for creating the task force, he said, was the sheer crush of supplicants asking for prayers of liberation.[13]

Representing a different school of thought is Father Gerald O'Collins, a Jesuit theologian, author, and professor at the Pontifical Gregorian University in Rome. "I do not want to exclude the possibility of demonic posses-sion," O'Collins said. "But I'm skeptical. It is too easy to rush in and blame demonic possession." While he sees a limited role in large dioceses for an exorcist—preferably an older, wise, and very holy priest—he does not think it should be a top priority. "I would get scared if I had sem-inary students who aspired to be exorcists," he said. "What would they think being a priest is about? It should be about helping old and young, administering the sacra-ments . . . teaching the word of God, and not going about exorcising demons."[14]

John Paul's last message for World Day of Peace, a major annual speech, focused again on fighting a palat-able evil. Troubled by what he called "violent fratricidal conflicts" raging in the world and especially in the Middle East, he made an impassioned plea for believers to over-come evil with good.

> From the beginning, humanity has known the tragedy of evil and has struggled to grasp its roots and to explain its causes. Evil is not some impersonal, deterministic force at work in the world. It is the result of human free-dom. Freedom, which distinguishes human beings from every other creature on earth, is ever present at the heart of the drama of evil.
>
> If we look to the present state of the world, we cannot help but note the disturb-ing spread of various social and political

manifestations of evil: from social disorders
to anarchy and war, from injustice to acts of
violence and killing. To steer a path between
the conflicting claims of good and evil, the
human family urgently needs to preserve and
esteem that common patrimony of moral values bestowed by God himself. . . . No man or
woman of good will can renounce the struggle to overcome evil with good.[15]

It was one of John Paul's final addresses. He died less
than four months later.

When Pope Benedict XVI was installed in April 2005,
it was unclear whether he would look upon exorcism
with as much favor as his predecessor. The former Joseph
Ratzinger of Germany is much more intellectual, eru-
dite, and, well, Germanic than John Paul, and he is far
less mystical. He had, after all, authored the recent restrictions on healing prayers.

But he is also a strict theological and political conservative, and he has frequently spoken of evil as an om-
nipresent and tangible threat eroding faith and morality
throughout the land. Benedict's primary goal is to recap-
ture Christian souls for the Catholic Church in an increasingly secular, godless world, and he apparently sees a role
for exorcists in that. To the delight and gratification of
many exorcists, he chose a public audience during the
first months of his papacy to praise a group of exorcists
who were meeting in the Umbria region of Italy at the

time as part of their annual convention. "I encourage you to pursue your important ministry in the service of the Church," Benedict told them, "sustained by the vigilant attention of your bishops and the unending prayer of the Christian community." His referring to their work as an "important ministry" seemed to represent a stamp of approval from the new pope.

Father Amorth took great comfort in the pope's endorsement. A supreme pontiff who understood the plight of the exorcists, he thought.

"It was very beautiful," he said.

"In the past, priests performing exorcisms fell into great error," Amorth acknowledged. "They unfortunately demonized people, people were tried as witches, and the possessed were burned at the stake. As a reaction to this craziness, everything was negated, even the very belief in the existence of the devil. Also the influence of lay currents of thought, especially rationalism and materialism, supported this tendency to stop believing in the devil and diabolical possession and evil spirits. It was no longer the moment for exorcists. I would have to say that the Roman Catholic Church, for three centuries, all but abandoned exorcism.

"Only starting again now, in the last couple of decades, has it come back." Amorth noted that there were 20 exorcists in Italy when he began in 1986, and today there are approximately 350.

"Now we have momentum."

CHAPTER IV

The Exorcists

For two years running now, the Regina Apostolorum Pontifical Athenaeum, a large new Vatican-affiliated university in Rome, has held a semester course for priests who want to become exorcists or who, at the minimum, want to learn more about the ritual and the phenomenon of demonic possession. Father Amorth still complains of resistance and a lack of support among some Church leaders, but he also welcomes what he says is a clear recognition at many levels of an acute shortage of the men able and willing to perform the task—and eagerness on the part of some elements of the hierarchy to do something to correct that situation.

This is particularly true at institutions like the Regina Apostolorum, which is run by the ultraconservative

Legionaries of Christ. The order claims 65,000 adherents and 600 priests worldwide.[1]

The school is located on the western outskirts of Rome, an expansive campus behind iron gates with wide green lawns; it almost looks as though it belongs in Southern California. The course the school offers is extensive. In ten day-long sessions over four months, a parade of exorcists, priests, sociologists, law enforcement officials, and other experts lecture a packed classroom on historical, theological, and pastoral aspects of exorcism and liberation prayer; on anthropological and sociological roots of belief in the devil; on psychological pathologies; and on the legal and juridical responses to Satanism and cults.

For these lectures, the Rome campus is hooked up by videophone with students and priests in Bologna, Milan, and other cities. Learning how to tell the difference between demonic possession and other psychological or physical traumas is one of the main goals of the program. The course ends with a round table during which Italy's leading exorcists, including Gabriele Amorth, discuss their experiences. Amorth did not participate the first year but joined the round table the second year. Most of the pupils are priests and some come from as far away as the Americas.

"The biggest obstacle has been the lack of training of priests and bishops, who haven't felt sufficiently equipped to confront [what the Church believes is a rising obsession with satanic cults, witchcraft, and the occult]," said

Giuseppe Ferrari, an academic with the Socio-Religious Research and Information Group, based in Bologna and a cosponsor of the course. "A deep and multidisciplinary formation should also fill the void felt especially by inexperienced and newly appointed exorcists, since they have lacked concrete preparation." In Turin, a northern Italian city that hosted the 2006 Winter Olympics, the archbishop recently ordered the dioceses' six exorcists to stop taking new cases until they have completed the course. Amorth praises these forums, coupled with the annual exorcists' convention, as important ways for aspiring exorcists to gain theoretical and practical insight and knowledge. Younger priests are also often called on to assist older exorcists in the rite as a way to get hands-on experience.

Thanks in large part to the Amorth-shepherded revival of Italian exorcism, more priests are training in how to identify the signs of diabolical intervention and how to safely administer the prayers of liberation.

"There is still resistance among the clergy; exorcism makes people uncomfortable. On a practical level, it is difficult to find priests willing to become exorcists. I think they are afraid. Fear that if they touch the demon, he will go after them. Leave the devil in peace, he will leave them in peace," Amorth said. "But I'm not worried. I still see, nevertheless, progress, and I think that will continue. I think the future is safe because I see that the number of exorcists continues to grow. There is a new generation of priests who really want to help people. They see there are so many requests from people who need and want to talk to an exorcist."

The Vatican's efforts to impose controls are met with varying degrees of enthusiasm. According to the rules, a bishop must always approve a full exorcism. Bishops, as managers of the Church, oversee priests and are answerable to the Vatican and, ultimately, the pope. Having the bishop's permission, then, is like having the imprimatur of the Church, which is backing that many, but not all, exorcists consider to be essential.

"Like you would do with specialists in a hospital emergency room, you don't want to overburden a single priest, so we try to spread the work around," said Monsignor Gabriele Cavina, a vicar, or senior official, in the archdiocese of Bologna. Among his tasks he oversees the city's ten exorcists, including Father Efrem, Caterina's exorcist. "To perform what we call the major exorcism, where the exorcist commands the devil to be gone, the exorcist always must have the permission of his bishop. You have to cover your back."

While shortages remain acute elsewhere in the world, like the United States, these days in Italy there is a bumper crop of exorcists, a new generation carrying forth the faith, even as the older masters continue to fight for acceptance and respectability. They have different styles and some bring more skepticism to the vocation than do others. Some are conflicted about the procedure, believing exorcism to be an answer of last resort. Others embrace it and appear as nonchalant about conducting an exorcism as a pharmacist is about doling out aspirin.

Here are profiles of four of today's exorcists, all of whom approach the ancient rite with very different attitudes and convictions.

The Dashing Exorcist

Fresh from a massive prayer ceremony in Portugal held at the site of the miracle of Fatima, exorcist Gabriele Nanni is eager to talk about his trade. Nanni is tall, thin, confident, and handsome. He has a thick head of salt-and-pepper hair and a trim beard to match. He is forty-six.

Nanni is also well-versed in the world of demons, a man for whom piety and bookish intelligence can coexist. He can quote chapter and verse on the history of Satan in the Bible. He produces documentaries and frequents the lecture circuit. And he is a star attraction at events like the exorcism course at the Regina Apostolorum. On a day journalists are allowed to attend, they crowd around him, flashing cameras in his face and sticking their microphones under his nose. Some of the women journalists gaze at him rather wistfully.

Nanni studied canon law at a pontifical university in Rome, has a doctorate in theology, worked in the Sacra Romana Rota (the top tribunal at the Vatican), and has served on the committee that studies whether a person is holy enough to be made a saint.

After moving a few years ago to Modena, a small city in northern Italy, he published a doctoral thesis on exorcism. "And from that moment my life changed," he said. "I am constantly on the move."

Being so very much in demand means less time for prayer. Nanni tries to limit his practice to a handful of difficult cases, including that of a thirty-five-year-old woman, an accountant with significant responsibilities at a commercial firm, who suddenly became overcome with asthma-like suffocation every time she attempted to enter a church. Her trouble began when she entered into an affair with her boss, who practiced black magic, Nanni said.

"We have to imagine a possessed person as a besieged town," Nanni said. "In an exorcism, thanks to the blessing, the evil spirit weakens and releases its grip. It is like an octopus holding an object tightly and, when the octopus begins to weaken, it has to release the object. But then it starts again to grip the object. This is a persistent action until the octopus is definitely defeated and it lets go, and the subject feels a complete relief."

Nanni is among those who tend to personify evil. He says today's theologians have made a serious mistake in declaring the devil dead, a notion that lures Catholics into dropping their guard.

"The devil is a person," Nanni says provocatively, challenging the more prevalent Church teachings. "If we refer to a person as a philosophic concept, an entity, a person having an identity, a way of thinking, a conscience. . . . God is a person. Three persons, actually. An angel is a person. The devil is a person. God is a person. Men are persons. Only animals are not to be considered persons. That's important because in this New Age culture, the animal is seen as a mixture, and that weakens the concept of person."

Not only is he a person, but the devil is also quite active. To make his point, Nanni cites the portrayal of Satan as a snake or serpent throughout the Bible—from the third chapter of Genesis ("Now, the serpent was more subtle than any other wild creature . . .") when he draws Eve into sin to the final book of the New Testament, Revelation, when he is "that ancient serpent, who is called the devil and Satan, the deceiver of the whole world" (Rev. 12:9, RSV). He thus earns the title of "the original murderer" from John the Evangelist. "The devil's aim is to strike every man," Nanni said. "His aim is not only to damage man's life on earth, but also to bring him, through suffering, to desperation and to the deepest sin against God. The devil is interested in an ordinary and extraordinary way in all human kind."

Nanni's bishop appointed him an exorcist in 2000. For two years before that, he attended a handful of exorcisms and watched or assisted elder priests performing the rite. He was kind of a self-styled apprentice, and he filled in for one of his mentors during summer vacation. He was intrigued by the phenomenon and it appealed to his sense of spiritual mission and the need to gently scare believers into a more faithful life. Like Amorth, he sees exorcism as a miracle, "an extraordinary intervention of God." He frequently officiates at mass prayer ceremonies, like the one at Fatima, that are dedicated to prayers of liberation but inevitably end in a small number of exorcisms. He said the afflicted are removed to smaller rooms so as to avoid public exposure and the possibility of "psychological contagion." At his last Fatima appearance, he co-officiated with an exorcist from Angola and an eighty-two-year-old Vietnamese priest living in exile in Paris.

While I saw Nanni at a couple of his public appearances, I finally caught up with him to have a sit-down talk over fruit-scented tea at his mother's home during a vacation. His mother helps him remember details of some of his cases. "Mamma," he will start, "you remember the one that . . . ." and she will fill in the blanks.

Only once, in his very first exorcism, was Nanni actually shocked. "Impressed" is the word he uses, but in Italian it has a stronger meaning. The patient was a middle-aged woman who remained silent in the exorcism and simply stared, her light-colored fixed eyes wide open. "She looked at me without moving even an eyelid," Nanni said. "She had such a cold glare. I have seen and heard worse things since, but that particular gaze, the way she looked at me. It was a stare so evil and icy, it is not easy to find."

Diabolic? I ask.

"Yes, without moving. Straight ahead. I was shocked."

Shocked? By a stare?

"The stare. The stare. Yes. I felt the strength of this

woman in her stare," Nanni said, recalling the moment. "I knew it was not human. There was resistance and an incredible wickedness. I mean, it was the first time I saw Satan's evil stare. He was looking at me."

Nanni's true primitive colors show vividly when he is speaking among his own. During the exorcists' round table at the conclusion of the Regina Apostolorum course, when no journalists or other outsiders were present, he spoke of his convictions that wizards and magicians, in secret pacts with the devil, place curses on good Christians. "From a statistical point of view, curses are the main cause of the suffering of so many people who go to exorcists," Nanni told the audience in Rome and those connected by videoconference. "The curse is made through demonic power that the wizard obtains through the rituals he follows through previous agreement with the demon, in which he venerates the demon and renounces the Christian faith."

To activate the curse by long distance, Nanni said, the sorcerer can use a fetish, a doll, or a photograph of the intended victim. If he has contact with the victim, he can use a form of satanic hypnosis, through a kind of penetrating stare that eventually subjugates the victim to his control. The curse is like a poison that courses through the victim's veins, sickens his mind, rots his body. Sometimes the curse causes cancer and tumors. Sometimes it feels like a moving animal is inside. "Sometimes you can see it, under the skin, in the abdomen and stomach area, an unexpected lifting up and down, like a snake or a frog," Nanni said. "The ensnared person is as though tied by an umbilical cord to the devil."

Ｔｈｅ Ｒｅｌｕｃｔａｎｔ Ｅｘｏｒｃｉｓｔ

The message flashes across his cellular telephone. A patient is telling Father Francois-Marie Dermine of two mosquito bites he suffered while at church. Overnight, they became swollen. "The pain was atrocious," the patient says via text message. Cortisone cream cured the terrible itching, thank goodness. A few weeks earlier, the same man sent a more ominous message to Dermine, a Dominican priest and the main exorcist in the Italian port city of Ancona. "I just want to thank you for everything," the patient said. "Maybe the place where I'm going will be better." Panicked, Dermine sprang into action and found the man just as he was about to down a bottleful of pills in an effort to end his life.

From insect bites to suicide, from the mundane to the potentially disastrous, this man clearly has a dependent relationship with his exorcist-priest—a dependency, actually, that puts enormous pressure on Dermine.

An all-consuming need on the part of patients is typical, and Dermine says the job is getting to him. He is depressed, practically forlorn. Dermine is something of an unwilling exorcist. His bishop asked him to take on the job several years ago, and Dermine complied. The bishop promised help, but that never materialized.

"There was a Capuchin friar, but he transferred out. There was another priest, but he was too shocked by the violence, and left. Priests don't want to do this. You have to sweat a lot. It's not easy. You have to learn alone. You have to gain experience alone."

And, he added, the demand is relentless. Day and night, disturbed people seek him out. They come to the door of the Dominican residence stuck discreetly on an Ancona street, blocks from the port. They beg for his help. It is endless.

"The phone never stops ringing," he said. His Dominican brothers who live with him know that the late-night knocks on the front door and the all-hours phone ringing are always for Dermine. Clad in the long, snowy white robe that is standard issue for Dominicans, Father Dermine, fifty-six, has sad eyes and a furrowed brow.

"I do this because I was forced—well, asked—by the bishop to take on this ministry. I know what it means. It means you have no peace. You live under siege," Dermine said. "Most who come to the exorcist don't need him. I don't see the devil everywhere. I try to look at God. But my experience is that many of the problems are not natural, that many of our problems do not have a natural cause."

The patient with the mosquito bites is a man in his thirties who has had an otherwise successful life. As

Dermine describes him, he is intelligent, a professor of lyrics at an Italian university, an accomplished musician, and a professional chef. Dermine believes he was, in fact, possessed, but that in the year and a half he's been working with him, the man has improved dramatically. He is still not free, however. The patient's principle affliction is what the exorcist calls *mediumship*: he has negative, sometimes awful premonitions that frequently come true, or seem to come true. Once he had a vision of hundreds of children being killed; a week later the tragedy at Beslan occurred, when rebels seized hostages at a school and nearly 1,000 people, mostly children, were killed or injured. It is as if the devil forces him to see terrible atrocities and death to torment him. The visions cause him to lose sleep, to be distracted from his normal activities, to become depressed, and as the mosquito bites showed, to become abnormally consumed by trivial problems.

In another case, a woman whose son died of a drug overdose was desperate to make contact with him in the afterlife. She attended a séance in which she supposedly made contact with her dead child. She went home and immediately began to hear voices, Dermine said. Aggressive, hostile voices spewing blasphemies and violence and cursing God and the saints. "I will kill you," the voices said. Father Dermine is now treating her, saying a series of blessings regularly, but he wonders, "You ask yourself, is she schizophrenic?" Often, he argues, a schizophrenic person cannot have a normal relationship with reality; by contrast, people who are vexed or possessed

often maintain normal lives, for periods of time, on many levels.

In another case that Dermine described, a thirty-two-year-old mother of two began hearing voices while at work in a hospital. They threatened to kill her and her children. She fell on the floor of the hospital and began flailing about. Doctors wanted to commit her, but she managed to control herself long enough to reach Dermine and the church. Hysterical, shouting, and fighting off the husband and sister who accompanied her, the woman entered the sanctuary. Dermine sat her before the altar and began to pray. After a few minutes of prayer, she began to rock back and forth with nearly inhuman speed, "like a windshield wiper." Four months later, Dermine was still working with her; she is better, but the voices have not gone away. "Liberation these days is taking much longer, and there are more cases," he said. "We don't understand why. Is it a lack of faith in ourselves? In the Church? In the priests? We have been lowering our guard."

Much of Dermine's practice is taken up with the blessing of houses and businesses. He has to perform one or two cleansing rituals every week at various places that have been cursed. People call him when there are mysterious flickerings of light, odd sounds, unexplained cracks in the walls, furniture that moves. And then there was the case of the footprints on the ceiling. "It's not quite like the movie *Poltergeist*," he said, "but it could be evil at work. I always ask if they've experienced any paranormal phenomena. Ninety percent of those who come are not truly possessed or even vexed. They just have a psychic disturbance."

Dermine recalled one instance in which a woman who owned a beauty parlor was threatened by an employee. The employee vowed to get rid of the owner and take over the business as her own. She placed a curse on the proprietor, and then things starting going haywire. One day a flame appeared in the beauty salon and burned the owner. Then a tube of dye jumped up and squirted itself all over the place. This, at least, is how the woman described events. Desperate, she called a police officer who, confounded, took her to Father Dermine. He prayed to the Holy Spirit and to the Virgin Mary on the woman's behalf, then sprinkled the beauty parlor with holy water and doused it with incense. He described the woman not as a hysterical type but as a balanced, pragmatic woman who is more reluctant than most to believe that evil spirits were at work. She was almost embarrassed by the whole episode, embarrassed to have to resort to an exorcist.

All of these phenomena could have perfectly normal explanations. That so many Italians see evil at work indicates an eagerness to pin blame on external factors; it is oddly reassuring on one level, a function of deep superstition on another. Part of the problem is that Italians by droves turn to fortune-tellers and magic and then become convinced that they are the victims of witchcraft or evil spells.

That trend is getting worse, Dermine believes. But he contends that part of the blame for people turning to the occult must rest with the Church itself. Too many priests are overly intellectual, disconnected from their flocks, and unwilling to take the time to listen. This at a time when many Catholics are seeking answers in a world adrift in chaos.

"People need certainties in their lives. They want to know if the other world exists. And people are coming less and less to church. We should examine our own consciences and ask ourselves why this is happening. People need something. Why?

"People are trying to find immediate solutions. No big religion offers an immediate solution but the so-called alternative religions do, as do magicians. With so much uncertainty . . . many people turn to magicians when they don't receive help from their priests, priests who are incompetent or who don't believe in demonic possession. Many priests think it's superstitious. Faith has become very intellectual; sometimes we are too intellectual in our way of living the faith."

Dermine parts company with Gabriele Amorth, Andrea Gemma, and some of the other old-school exorcists and frowns on the use of the exorcism as a diagnosis. Using the rite in that way should be avoided, he says. It creates a dangerous dependence on the ceremony itself, in which the patient will never understand that the prayers of liberation or of exorcism are but the start of a process of healing. If you start with an exorcism, without having exhausted medical and other therapeutic possibilities, the patients believe only in exorcism and are then unwilling to confront their problems in other ways. It takes away their responsibility and allows them to blame the devil too readily. In this way, the abuse of exorcism can be as harmful as magic.

And on occasion, Dermine said, sick people trying to get the attention of their families will "pathologically simulate" the supposed trance of the possessed person, in a "perverse process of shirking responsibility."

For Father Dermine, one of the most troubling and horrific cases of his career as an exorcist involved ministering to a ten-year-old boy who claimed to have been victimized by a notorious satanic sect in Bologna known as the Bambini di Satana—Satan's Children. Although abuse during a spooky series of alleged satanic rituals was never proven, and a court case eventually fell apart, the boy suffered some sort of trauma, Dermine said. He developed a fierce aversion to all things holy and became very fearful of priests. He was not possessed but certainly screwed up. His parents eventually sought help from the police and then from Dermine, who began praying with him. Over time, he calmed and, while still fragile, has largely recovered.

Dermine first consulted an exorcist thirty years ago—for a suicidal girl he was counseling—while studying to become a priest. He is a professor of moral theology with a degree in political science. To this day, he remains astonished, and disturbed, by the things he's seen. "I always believed in the existence of the devil and his actions. But I never thought that I would confront concrete proof.

"It is very, very dark. The people. The cases you confront, the things people tell you. The actions of the devil on people. Suffering is always mysterious. You have no explanation. Why does God allow these things? You have only to pray."

The Senior Exorcist

Monsignor Andrea Gemma is the only bishop in Italy who is also an official exorcist. That ranking gives him a clout unparalleled in the world of demon-bashing; he calls himself "a rare beast." Italians come from all over the country to the southern town of Isernia, where he serves, to seek out his blessing. Isernia is typical of Italy's south, poor but religious. People who pass casually by the cathedral in the center of town do not fail to cross themselves. The town has about 60,000 residents—and five exorcists.

Gemma is not shy about criticizing those in the Church hierarchy who are less than enthusiastic about exorcisms. He cheerfully adheres to the old ways and chafes at restrictions that the Church has more recently tried to impose, including the requirement that priests consult with doctors before submitting a patient to an exorcism. The exorcism itself is the best way to determine a diagnosis, Gemma argues—a controversial point in today's Church but an opinion he shares with Father Amorth. He dismisses the suggestion that resorting too readily to exorcism could lead to abuse. "An exorcism, above all, is prayer, and prayer cannot do harm," said Gemma, who considers The Lord's Prayer—"deliver us from evil"—the most beautiful exorcism in the world. "I am not interested in the diagnosis that the doctor does. What can an expert tell us? What can a psychologist say, what can a psychiatrist say, when confronted by a phenomenon that is very far outside his competence? He cannot say anything. The most he could do is give a diagnosis that is negative, saying, 'Here I can do nothing, here I can say nothing.' That's the only thing a psychiatrist or a psychologist would be able to do. Therefore, I am firmly convinced of the diagnostic value of the exorcism."

Enza, a thirty-six-year-old woman with thick, shoulder-length brown hair, arrives for her weekly exorcism.

Gemma has been working with Enza for three or four years, and for several years before that she saw other exorcists. She has gradually improved slightly, but she has a long way to go. The unemployed, stocky-built daughter of a retired bricklayer, Enza still lives at home. As she walks into the marble halls of the Isernia Cathedral, dressed in black and wearing sunglasses despite the winter grayness, she staggers and begins to breathe heavily. "Calm down, calm down," say her sister and mother, who accompany her. She clutches a plastic bag of medicines that she uses, evidently to keep a grasp on sanity. She deposits the bag on a table and enters the salon where Gemma will exorcise her. She stretches out on an upholstered couch under a portrait of the Madonna, her mother and sister at each end. Gemma, wearing the purple skullcap of the bishopric and a large, heavy gold cross on a chain around his neck, begins with a rosary: "In the name of the Father, the Son, and the Holy Spirit. . . Hail Mary, full of grace . . . God, pray with us . . ."

Gemma permits me to listen to the exorcism from outside the closed doors but not to watch. It is 9:25 on a Wednesday morning.

The voice that hurtles from Enza is mostly masculine, angry, and exceedingly vulgar. Within minutes she convulses into a series of guttural, vomiting sounds. And then: "I hate you! I hate you!" she screams. "Basta, basta! Leave me alone!" Gemma continues calmly with a steady murmur of prayer, invoking saints, Jesus, and the Mother of God, Santa Maria. "Fuck you, asshole!" the voice screams, deep and harsh. "You're busting my balls! I hate you! Leave me alone!"

"Dio onnipotente. God Almighty . . ."

Enza lapses into repeated grunts that sound like enormous burps. "I hate you!" she shouts over and over.

"Hate me more!" Gemma challenges, adding, "God loves Enza! He loves her because she was baptized. She was confirmed. Enza is a good person!"

"I don't give a fucking damn," Enza thunders back. "What the fuck do I care?"

Then, "Shut up," she hisses, spitting at the priest. He continues to pray and she screams endlessly, with such force that the voice becomes unrecognizable as anything human. It reverberates through the hallway.

"Holy Father, exorcise," Gemma says. "Saint Michael and all the angels who are in front of you . . ."

"*Ahhhhhhhhh!*"

"Holy apostles. . . ."

"Bastaaaaa! Enough!"

"Holy Father, answer the prayers of Saint Peter and Saint Paul . . . Blessed be the Lord . . . Blessed be Jesus Christ . . ."

"You are disgusting!" the voice in Enza shrieks.

"*You* are disgusting, you are disgusting," Gemma retorts. "Be ashamed!"

Enza becomes increasingly vulgar, using words for human testicles that don't have translations in English. She repeats the litany over and over—I hate you! Shut up! Leave me alone!

"Padre Pio," Gemma says, invoking one of southern Italy's favorite saints, "pray for us. Padre Pio, pray for us."

"I don't give a shit," Enza responds. "Stop it!"

"Louder!"

"*Stop it!*"

After about twenty minutes of screaming, Gemma turns to Latin. "Immondissime spiritus, in nomine dei patris, et filii et spiritus sancti," he prays. "Caede deos, caede filio dei, da locus spirituri santo, da locus spirituri santo . . ."

Enza returns to bursts of burping groans.

"In the name of God, go away!" Gemma commands.

"Stick it up your ass," Enza responds.

Gemma begins his interrogation of the demon possessing Enza. "When are you leaving?"

"Never!"

"Why not?"

"Because I don't want to."

"Who sent you to enter Enza's body?"

"I am who entered."

"Why did you enter her?"

"Because Enza was too good."

"Because Enza was too good? She is still a good person. And she will return to being a good, serene, and calm person. And you will go because God will force you to!"

Monsignor Gemma takes a crown from a statue of the Madonna and places it on Enza's head. She contorts. "The Madonna squashed your head!" Gemma declares with satisfaction.

"Coward!" the young woman screams back.

"Tell the truth, the Madonna squashed you!"

"No, no! It's not fucking true!"

"It *is* true! You are a liar. You are scared . . . you are scared. Scared of the Madonna! Kiss the crown!"

Enza launches into ten long screams, the kind that curdle the blood and chill the bones. "Damn you, you bastard, you will pay for this!" she finally booms.

"I exorcise you," Gemma begins again, and again in

Latin: "Immondissime spiritus, in nomine dei patris, et filii . . ."

"You're busting my balls!"

"Are you leaving, yes or no?" Gemma again demands.

"Basta! Basta! Basta!" the voice moans. Now Enza begins to sob.

"Do not cry, Enza," the priest consoles. "God loves you."

"You are a pig," says Enza. "I want to die. I want you to die."

At this point, exactly half an hour after he began—though it seems like much more time has passed—the exorcist decides to let Enza rest. He walks out of the room, leaving her with her mother and sister. They can be heard praying quietly, then imploring their tormented daughter and sibling to return to them. "Wake up, wake up, come back to yourself," the sister says. "God is alive. He is not dead."

"Whores! Sluts! Bastards!" Enza growls in response. "Go away! Christ is dead and so are all the saints."

"Come back, come back," the other women implore.

After a few more minutes of quiet prayer, Gemma returns to Enza. She is calm now. She kisses the golden bishop's ring on his right hand. The exorcism is over.

Enza appears exhausted, wrung out like a dishrag. Her eyes are swollen from crying. Her mother and sister wipe her face. They slowly pick up their belongings, straighten themselves, and go home, Enza stepping heavily, leaning against her sister for support.

Gemma explains later that Enza is one of his most difficult cases, a rare example of true demonic possession. Not only does her voice change during the rite, so does her face; her gaze locks into a vacant stare, and she never looks directly at the priest. "You can see that she is transformed; it is no longer her talking, it is him inside her." In addition to becoming masculine, the voice shifts pitch and tone and sounds like several different people. And it curses with a bawdy language that Enza does not use.

"In this case, since this poor woman has the terrible habit of spitting, spitting in your face, I keep at a distance from her," Gemma said. "Also when I impose my hands on her body, I take cover behind the mother. The exorcist has to watch out for himself. Early on, this poor woman tried to throw that little table at me."

Gemma suspects Enza became possessed because her parents were frequenting magicians and fortune-tellers, which he says is one of the most common ways the devil attacks his victims. Either the target or the target's parents or relatives get involved in black magic, and the door is open. "The first boy I exorcised, a certain Luigi, had become possessed through a séance that was performed at his school. His school!" Gemma said. At the very start with Enza, her parents had to come clean. "They were practicing many occult things," Gemma explained. "After my very first meeting with them, the first thing I told them was they had to confess these sins they had committed, because it goes against God's law, and then promise never to go back to the magicians." Only then did Gemma take on their daughter as a patient.

Enza's mother, in a separate interview, insisted she tried to do the best by her daughter, who began to fall ill a couple of years after graduating from high school. Initially she worked for a Catholic youth group, but then quit. She complained to her family that she was not feeling well. "But we didn't understand," the mother said. Finally, they took her to a doctor who diagnosed a thyroid condition and gave her medicine. A second doctor said there wasn't a thing wrong with her thyroid and recommended discontinuing the medicine. Nothing seemed to help. Enza deteriorated. As her mother described it, she became overly sensitive to noise and insisted on remaining in a darkened room, or sleeping for long periods. She'd refuse meals with the family, leave the home, and disappear for hours. And then there were the screaming fits. A cousin told her to pray to Jesus. Enza responded, "The more I pray, the worse I feel."

They took Enza to a psychologist, but that didn't help either. Finally, they turned to the exorcists. As improvement is measured in these things, Enza has improved. Where it once took five men to hold her down during an exorcism, Enza can now be sufficiently restrained by her mother and sister alone. Still, she frequently turns violent in the evening, at the time of late afternoon Catholic prayers. Enza is not able to carry on a normal life, socialize with friends, or hold down a job. Sometimes she convulses in bed or breaks furniture; one time she ran away and tried to kill someone. The police captured her. When her parents showed up at the station and explained that she was possessed, the police said that in such a case, the parents were responsible for keeping her locked up at home.

"You can't imagine what the devil makes her do. For five minutes, it's Enza, and then the next five minutes, she is someone else. It's like a split personality," the mother said. The family is simple, of modest means and limited education, from Italy's less sophisticated south. No one in the family ever learned to drive a car. "I don't know who did such an evil thing to us," the mother said. "I just cried and cried to see my daughter like that."

Gemma says it could take years to cure Enza, if she is ever cured. Only in one case did he see an immediate "liberation," as the exorcists call it. He said it was like the person was a balloon and all the air suddenly exited. "I'm free," the person said. Normally, liberation takes months or years, he said. And rarely does it happen in the exorcist's presence, but rather in an intimate "moment of grace."

"Do not think that possession is something you get rid of in a short time. The devil will laugh at you if you think that a little sprinkle [of holy water] will do it. It lasts as long as God wants."

He spoke of his most recent triumph. Just a couple of months earlier, a woman patient from Venice, in northern Italy, abruptly became free. She was before an image of the Virgin Mary when she suddenly felt cured. She returned to Gemma and asked to take Communion. Previously, she had never been able even to enter the church without great difficulty, and here she was, asking for the Eucharist, the holiest of sacraments. Gemma was nervous, knowing how disruptive a possessed person can be in the middle of a Mass. But he took the chance, and sure enough, she was fine. She took the host (wafer) and wine, which Catholics believe literally to be the body and blood of Christ, and then embraced Gemma. "And then I knew she was finally liberated," Gemma said, becoming a bit emotional as he told the story for the first time to outsiders. "It was very beautiful, very beautiful. And now she takes Holy Communion every day. I experienced the joy of seeing this lady liberated in an unexpected way. This was a wonderful consolation that repays me for all of these other difficulties."

As the woman from Venice illustrates, patients come from all over Italy to seek out Gemma. That is why Isernia has five exorcists, to help the bishop contend with so many troubled souls (and not, Gemma says with a hearty chuckle, because there is more evil in Isernia than other locations). In part, it's the fact of his rank. "When a big shot like me is listening, it makes them feel better," he said. But it is also the mere fact that he listens, something in short supply in many dioceses, he says.

"I tell them to go to their own bishop, but they often tell me that those who have been appointed exorcists are the first ones who don't believe it. Some laugh at it. They mock it and think it's been blown out of proportion.

"So finding someone who listens and prays is important, even psychologically. Sometimes just the fact of being listened to, of being invited into prayer and into a relationship of trust, this is a great remedy for those who are suffering."

Gemma, seventy-four, speaks at times with a slow, dramatic flair, repeating his words for emphasis. Yet he is also not afraid to joke and laugh. He was a much-heralded opening act at the most recent exorcism course at the Regina Apostolorum, where he regaled the priests with his stories, his eagerness to knock down the mystique around diabolical possession, and his penchant for the closest thing to irreverence that a bishop can muster when talking about Church hierarchy.

He doesn't take the devil too seriously: "I always say, the best thing is to make fun of the devil. You cannot give much weight to what he says. We fear the devil, but we have to minimize him."

He believes the new rite is unrealistic and too timid: "Why does the Holy See not trust us bishops?" he complained to the class.

And he says the Church generally gives short shrift to crucial traditions like the use of Latin, part of what Gemma thinks is a global plot to undermine Christianity: "The devil is happy with the near-disappearance of Latin."

His specific bone of contention is the stress that the new rite puts on medical consultation. "The exorcism itself allows us to distinguish who needs an exorcism and who doesn't. When one has no need for it, he comes the first time and never returns again. Who does need it, by contrast, comes back. He needs blessings. He needs to return.

"Often I may not be able to make the diagnosis, but I have the medicine that is good for every illness. And the medicine that is good for every illness is prayer. Maybe I can't always make the best diagnosis, but my remedy always serves: prayer and exorcism."

Gemma went public with his decision to become an exorcist in a pastoral letter to his diocese dated June 29, 1992, about eighteen months after he was ordained a bishop. Titled "The Gates of Hell Will Not Prevail" (a quote from the Gospels), the letter was candidly direct in arguing the presence of demons and the need to proactively eradicate them. Gemma calls the letter "the most important of my bishopric," saying it was "extraordinary and unusual" and generated a lot of commentary.

"As Pope John Paul II puts it, Satan's infestation actions are dark and, believe me, far more dispersed than you could ever think or believe," Gemma wrote. "The sarcastic skepticism among the world's pseudo-thinkers, and even among some Christians and religious teachers, is the fruit of disinformation and, therefore, superficiality, which becomes the very basis for the victory that the Evil One wishes to obtain, covered in silence. I call on all the pastors of God's people: no one should treat this lightly! . . . Everyone must be disposed to healthy discernment, as a kind of pastoral duty, but never, never,

never can it be treated with superficiality, minimizing the problems, or worse, refusing to listen to it. That is not how Jesus did it!"

Gemma then offered a few guidelines for exorcists and exorcisms, something he believes any priest can be and can perform. First, unity and communion are important among men of God and people of faith, because such spirituality keeps evil away. The devil is hate and division, Gemma wrote, and he cannot thrive where communion exists. This is why joint prayer and prayers of liberation recited in unison are particularly effective. Evoking the Virgin Mary is also especially important, because she is Satan's eternal enemy. And, he cautioned, the person receiving the blessing must be open to it, must have renounced sin, and recurred to prayer and the sacraments; otherwise, the blessing might as well be an amulet.

"My brothers, did you understand?" Gemma wrote. "I am calling on my entire Church to rally behind a war without quarter, simultaneous, efficient, against evil and its many branches."

After he issued the letter, Gemma started with regular sessions of liberation prayers in which large groups would gather in the Isernia Cathedral to pray for liberation. At the end of these sessions, however, he saw more and more people who clearly needed extra attention—actual exorcisms. They were screaming or in pain or otherwise tormented. Nowadays, the group liberation is done the last Saturday of every month.

And so, for the last thirteen years, Gemma says he has been performing five exorcisms a week. In that time, he figures he has encountered ten people suffering from true demonic possession.

"When an exorcist tells you this—only ten possessions in thirteen years—it tells you very clearly that I do not see the devil everywhere."

†he Controversial Exorcist

Perhaps no one has done more harm to the image of the exorcist than Archbishop Emmanuel Milingo. Born in a village in Zambia, what was then Northern Rhodesia, Milingo was ordained a priest in 1958 and was named bishop of Lusaka, the capital of Zambia, eleven years later. The Vatican stripped him of the archbishopric and ordered him to Rome nearly two decades ago, and he has lived in Italy ever since. He was never officially designated as an exorcist and instead performs healing masses and exorcisms according to his own energetic, eccentric style, based on what he considers to be the duty and responsibility of any man of God. As he puts it, "I am an exorcist not by appointment but by faith."

His habit of following his own rules on exorcisms is not the only thing that has landed him in trouble with the Vatican. In 2001 he shocked the Catholic world by marrying Marie Sung, a Korean acupuncturist who belonged to the Reverend Sun Myung Moon's Unification Church.

They married in a mass wedding officiated by Moon in New York. Less than three months later, following pressure from the Vatican, threats of excommunication, and a private plea from then-pope John Paul II, Milingo came to his senses, repented, and renounced his marriage. He returned to the fold and went into seclusion. Early in the scandal, he said he was making a point about his belief that the Church should end its celibacy requirements and allow for married priests. But later, after the scandal subsided, he wrote in a book that the entire episode may have been the result of his having been brainwashed. The events did little to enhance his credibility.

Milingo's more enduring troubles with the Church hierarchy date back much further. From his early days as a bishop in Zambia, he performed raucous healing masses and public exorcisms that uneasy Church critics said smacked of voodooism. His critics saw him as plain wacky. He was repeatedly warned by Vatican officials to cease, and he repeatedly ignored the warnings. Even when the Vatican decided it had had enough and yanked him to Rome, Milingo continued his exotic priestly practice for Italian audiences. Thousands of Catholics from all over Italy—and even farther afield—flocked to his monthly sessions, which were held initially in a church in suburban Rome and later in warehouses, stadiums, and assorted venues. And he continued even as several Italian bishops banned him from their dioceses.

The Moonie marriage episode slowed Milingo down. He was bundled off to a small town, Zagarolo, about a ninety-minute drive south of Rome. After an interlude, however, he returned to what he still considers his rightful ministry. In a barrack-size white tent inside his Zagarolo compound, Milingo resumed healing ceremonies to pray for the sick and, when necessary, cast out demons from followers who seek him out every week. It seemed that he and the Vatican reached a quiet understanding. Church officials never really wanted to excommunicate him because of an institutional reluctance on the part of the Vatican to purge one of its own. In addition, officials feared Milingo's following was so great that he would take a segment of the Church with him if he left.

Milingo, in turn, became slightly more measured in his public comments and more discreet in his theatrics. Tolerance of him, he said, reflects wider acceptance in the Church of exorcism.

"There has been a big change of attitudes toward the healing ministry," he said one day at his office. "There has been great progress in the understanding of the Church itself, toward preaching the Gospel but also protecting and feeding the sheep. The understanding has really made great strides in the Church today. Not only is Milingo allowed to do his work publicly today, but there are many parishes and there are many priests who now have time for casting out the devils and healing the sick, once a week."

For all his flamboyance, Milingo seemed a personable man, friendly and welcoming, very devout. At Zagarolo, Milingo was living and working in a large, secluded compound shrouded in Mediterranean evergreens and protected by an electronic wrought iron gate half covered in chicken wire. Not easy to find. But many people do. A long sloping driveway leads to the three-story yellow-trimmed house where his office and sleeping quarters are. Several black African nuns in colorful headscarves and matching long skirts normally attend to him, washing his clothes, cooking his meals, and keeping his appointment book. He calls this place a Spirituality Center. In a field next to the house is the white tent, as well as a bank of vending machines offering Cokes and candy bars and a couple of Porta Potties. There is also a small bookshop and gift store selling rosaries and a panorama of prayer books with Milingo's picture on the covers.

On one autumn Thursday in 2005, people have been arriving all day long. The front gate is open and the cars parade steadily up the driveway and line up in a gravel-covered parking lot. By the time Mass starts at around 2:30, there are several hundred people. Judging from their license plates, they have come from as far away as the northern coast and the southern area around Naples. Older men and women, couples with little children, entire families. Women in smart pantsuits and others with bad hair-dye jobs and too much makeup; kids with backpacks; a very small number of mentally retarded and physically crippled.

"I come to encounter Jesus," says one older, rotund man as he steps up to the tent. "It's like telling jokes. Not everyone can tell a good joke. Not everyone can show you Jesus." A twenty-six-year-old woman with a nose ring and tight blue jeans, pushing her two-year-old daughter in a stroller, says she's been coming almost every week for four years. It makes her feel better. "When I don't come, everything bad happens," she says.

As they approach the tent, scores of people stop at a metal spigot and fill plastic bottles and jugs with water. Milingo will bless the water, as well as other items people bring, including family photographs, rosaries, and candles, during the ceremony. Milingo's helpers also give out tickets with numbers to those in attendance; you are allowed to approach for your individual blessing only when your number is called, like at the butcher shop.

They will be there, inside the tent, for nearly four hours. Milingo and a team of priests will lead them in incessant prayer, and endless song will be led by a choir of four women in melodious a cappella harmony. The priests send puffs of incense floating through the congregation. The altar, at the far end of the tent, sits under a large crucifix. A life-size statue of Christ on the cross, his jagged heart exposed, stands on one side of the altar, a shrine to Mary on the other. One priest stays in a corner, to the left of the altar, hearing a parade of confessions. A young man wearing a denim jacket and clutching a wooden rosary seems particularly troubled; the priest spends a long time with him, holding his face in his hands, patting his cheeks, insisting on something.

The Mass opens traditionally enough, with hymns and prayers, and evolves to a ceremony cast in Milingo's style. There is a lot of kneeling and rousing clap-along to the songs, one of which praises the Black Madonna. Milingo, at one point, strides down the center aisle sprinkling holy water from an aspergillum onto worshippers who hold aloft their family photos or bow deeply and cross themselves.

In a sermon delivered in heavily accented Italian and wildly scattered syntax, Milingo tells his congregation that the devil has helped to cause sin in man, but that men must also own up to their own responsibility and turn to God to live in peace and happiness.

"We have to measure our words, our way of acting, our life, and our relations with people. For example, if Milingo doesn't pray to God, I can't help you. It's through God that he makes me know you, and I make myself useful so that I can help you," he preaches. Milingo has a tendency to speak of himself in both the third and first person, often in the same sentence.

"So, sometimes people come here and ask: 'Is Milingo here?' Why do they come to Milingo? Like Jesus said, you have to live the problems, it's not just puff, puff and it's gone." It's not clear that everyone really understands what Milingo is saying, but it doesn't matter. The message seems personal and pious, and they cheer and applaud him.

After the sermon, the prayers build up in a crescendo toward passionate pleas for salvation from evil and healing from ills both physical and spiritual. "Oh Jesus

Savior," they recite in unison, with Milingo in the lead, "I pray you free me from every influence of evil . . ."

To the Virgin Mary: "Oh Queen of Heaven and Sovereign of the Angels, to you who received from God the mission of crushing the head of Satan, we humbly ask you to send your celestial legions, because at your command they will chase the demons, combating them everywhere, repressing their audacity and driving them back to the abyss."

To Saint Michael: "Defend us in battle, be our protector against the wickedness and snares of the devil . . ."

Just as Milingo invokes Pope Leo XIII's prayer to Michael the Archangel, he invokes the late pope's exorcism prayer. "Go, Satan, inventor and master of deceit, enemy of the salvation of man! Give way to Christ, give way to the Church that Christ acquired with his blood."

As the celebration reaches a fever pitch, some in the audience are shouting these prayers. A red-haired woman with a tic begins to twitch uncontrollably. An old man in the second row moans and writhes on the ground. And so it goes. (I am told later that this was nothing. Some Thursdays it's downright scary, says one young woman. "I've learned not to turn around when I hear the screams," she confides.)

"Liberate us!" Milingo intones. "Heal us! In the name of the Father, the Son, and the Holy Ghost! Amen!" The congregation shouts "Amen" in response and breaks into wild applause. There is a release of sorts. The worshippers have reached their peak of reverence and calm down. In a few minutes, they file obediently through the aisles to take Communion. The Mass is over, and now it's time for the laying on of hands.

Milingo's helpers call the numbers in batches. When their number is called, worshippers line up, two by two, in front of Milingo, who is now seated in an upholstered chair in front of the altar.

Guards who look a little like bouncers stand watch. Two women are positioned on either side of Milingo, and two men stand at the head of the line of people waiting to see him. They guide the faithful in pairs to Milingo, help them kneel before him (push them in a few cases), and then lift and move them along. Milingo says a brief prayer for each man, woman, or child and places his hand on their foreheads and sometimes on the side of their heads as well. For the more troubled cases he spends an extra minute or so. Some people say a few words to him or ask for a special prayer for a loved one who is sick. A placid look descends onto the face of one older woman, and she keels over. Several other women have to be held up as they stagger away, overcome.

It is only at this point, at the end of hours of ritual, that possessed people might show themselves, Milingo says, and he will perform an exorcism. Today there is only one candidate. A chestnut-haired woman of about thirty, well-known to Milingo's staff, approaches. During the Communion, she had waited until the last moment and then winced when one of the priests placed the wafer in her mouth. Suddenly weak, she had to be helped to one side of the tent, where someone sat with her. Now, at the conclusion of the laying on of hands, she has again waited. Milingo places his hands on her head. She writhes in terrible pain, then collapses as if she has fainted. The priest prays and the aides call the woman's name. She revives but then recoils again. The guards lift her and take her to a chair, where she sits for a long time. A woman who works for Milingo sits by her side and embraces her.

† † †

The healing masses presided over by Milingo became so outlandish in the 1980s and 1990s that the Church felt compelled to rewrite the rules. He was presiding over what amounted to public exorcisms, allowing them to be filmed and maintaining the decorum befitting a traveling salesman. The Church clamped down in 2000. Healing ceremonies had to be conducted outside of and apart from the regular Mass, the Church said in new guidelines, and had to be authorized by a bishop, even if the celebrant was a bishop. The measures were clearly aimed at Milingo. In addition, it was Joseph Ratzinger, the Church's doctrinal watchdog, who was in charge of reprimanding Milingo after his Moonie marriage. Since Ratzinger has been elevated to Saint Peter's throne, one might think Milingo would feel threatened that his former nemesis now controls the vast Roman Catholic Church.

Initially, at least, that did not appear to be the case. While more subdued than in the past, Milingo continued to emphasize the importance of healing and exorcism, all as part of the comprehensive, holistic approach to preaching the word of God.

"With a healing ministry you heal not only the symptoms of the malaise but you are also making the person become more resistant so that he knows how to combat them," Milingo said. "Some people who come here have very sad stories. We assure them that God never abandons those he created.

"We calm them," he continued. "We pray together. They are living continuously in tension. The Lord gives them time to reflect. He gives them hope. Instead of feeling vanquished, instead of pointing fingers at one another, through prayer we let them become calm and interdependent.

"The casting out of devils is something that is delicate, very delicate," he went on. "The so-called possessed persons are not to be condemned as though they are already in hell and their lives are being controlled by the devil. That is completely wrong. Even exorcists sometimes treat them as if they are culpable of what they have become. It is not as though they have collaborated with the devil and find themselves in this position. Not at all. We must deal with them as the Lord himself would deal with his sheep. You are a shepherd who sees the lion, the wolf, the hyena. The shepherd has reason to chase these ferocious animals. Even if some of your flock is not liv-

ing in peace, they are disturbed. We must go in search of
the lost sheep. Each and every one is saved by the blood
of Christ."

Milingo emphasized that one cannot concentrate on
exorcisms alone. Everyone needs protection, even if that
requires nothing more than a simple prayer or blessing.
Consequently, in addition to his Thursday healing cele-
brations, Milingo was seeing a steady procession of troubled people all week long. They sought him out, people
with bad marriages, problematic children, or sickness.
The remorseless. Sufferers and sinners. The devil, he
says, manifests himself in myriad terrible ways.

When he does confront the devil—and Milingo says
he has many times—he is ready. "I say to him, 'You have
no right to be here! I throw you at the feet of Jesus and
send you back to hell.' That's what I tell the devil. There
is a wise way to have a conversation with the devil. I ask
him where he came from, under whose authority, and
how long he plans to stay. It is imprudent to enter into a
longer conversation."

At the end of a long conversation with Milingo, he
took me aside to say something that essentially sums up
his philosophy and illustrates his fundamental divergence
from official Vatican handling of exorcisms. To really understand this work, he cautioned, speak to the spiritual-
ists, not the theologians. In other words, feel it through
faith and mysticism. Don't try to understand it through
intellectual application. Feeling, not rules.

Several months after my last meeting with Milingo,

he again shocked and consternated the Vatican. He turned up in Washington, D.C., and gave a news conference in which he advocated lifting celibacy rules for priests.[2] There were rumors that he was reunited with his wife. The Vatican wasted no time in taking the unusual step of issuing a highly critical statement, saying that if the comments attributed to Milingo were true, the Church could only "deplore" such a departure from "well-known" teachings. And then came the final straw, as far as the Vatican was concerned. In September 2006, Milingo, still in Washington, attempted to ordain four married men as bishops. Declaring the African archbishop was "spreading division and confusion among the faithful," the Vatican immediately excommunicated him, a severe punishment that barred Milingo from taking part in public worship. His crime, in the Church's view, was to attempt an ordination without papal approval. Milingo had again broken, perhaps irrevocably this time, with what he viewed as the confines of Rome.

If exorcism were the exclusive purview of people like Milingo, marginalized from the Church's perspective—a cleric who looms on the fringes—then it might be easier to dismiss. But Milingo is the extreme in a cult with wider acceptance and higher backing.

CHAPTER V

Patients

While the statistics are fuzzy, it appears that far more women than men are seeking and undergoing exorcisms. Women may simply be more willing to talk about it than men, especially in a society that is still relatively *machista*, like Italy. But judging from extensive interviews with exorcists, the bulk of their patient load consists of women.

A number of psychologists argue that the preponderance of women patients is only the latest in a long history of phenomena in which women are considered to be the focus of evil. In the Judeo-Christian tradition this goes as far back as Adam and Eve. Eve tempted Adam and brought sin upon him. "For Adam was formed first, then Eve; and Adam was not deceived, but the woman was deceived and became a transgressor" (1 Timothy 2:13–14,

RSV). Woman is to blame for the fall of man. The devil does his work through the woman. Men are inherently weak when it comes to women and, try as they might, they fall to temptation when it comes to women. In many societies it is the responsibility of the woman to be chaste and not use her powers to ruin men. This thinking goes beyond Christianity. In some Islamic cultures, for example, the woman must cover herself with veils, scarves, and robes so as not to tempt the man, who simply cannot control himself. Failure is the woman's fault; for any sexual transgression, she will be punished, not necessarily the man, because, poor thing, he could not help himself—he could not resist. It reaches the extreme of instances in which women who are raped are blamed for the crime and punished with death.

Then, hysteria—and it is clear that some portion of the belief in demonic possession is related to hysteria—has always been more readily associated with women. The word comes from *hyster*, Greek for womb. The ancient Greeks believed that "hysteria" was a condition caused by abnormalities involving the uterus. By its modern definition, hysteria, better known now as conversion disorder, is the phenomenon whereby repressed psychological (or sexual) disturbances manifest themselves as imaginary physical illnesses, such as paralysis, blindness, or convulsive fits. Through history, women have been the chief protagonists of periods of mass hysteria. From the fifteenth century through the seventeenth century (and in a number of cases, as late as the middle of the eighteenth century), Europe was awash in persecutions of supposed witches accused in trials of black magic, blasphemy, and consorting with the devil. Catholic and Protestant churches had a hand in the persecutions, but so did the secular authorities of the day. The witch hunts, interestingly enough, were rampant in northern European countries like Germany, England, and Sweden and far less commonplace in Italy and Spain. One theory is that where the faith was secure, strong, and unchallenged, like fervently Catholic Italy, paranoia was less likely to seize the populace. The notorious Spanish Inquisition, some historians now say, executed only a fraction of those condemned before it. By contrast, elsewhere in Europe, tens of thousands of people were "convicted" of being witches or warlocks and executed by hanging, by burning at the stake, or through other gruesome forms of capital punishment.

An enormous percentage of the accused, and most of those executed, were women. When colonial America experienced its own witch craze in the 1690s in Salem, Massachusetts, most people executed as witches were women. There are numerous reasons for this. If the devil is seen in masculine terms, then it is obvious that he can assert his will sexually over a woman. And many puritans of the day feared women and the sexuality that women represented. Women in Renaissance Europe served in roles that lent themselves to being accused of evil-doing; midwives, for example, were often accused of witchcraft if the baby died, and babies died frequently in those days.

Again, well into the eighteenth and nineteenth centuries, before scientific knowledge was commonplace, odd behavior was often blamed on the workings of God and Satan.

Father Amorth says he has noticed the trend of women patients outnumbering men, and while he has a few theories, he is at a loss to understand it completely.

"I maintain that in part, the reason is because women are the ones who do the most praying. Another reason is women are more inclined to approach a priest than are men, in case of need," Amorth said. "And another reason is women are more at risk for demonic influence because it is women who more readily turn to magicians and witches and fortune-tellers and séances and satanic sects. Well, not so much satanic sects, which is more men." It is the resorting to the occult that "opens the door" to demonic possession, Amorth maintains.

"And another reason," he continued. "Satan hates the Madonna. Hatred of the Madonna translates into hatred of women, and through hatred of the woman he can get at the man. None of this convinces me totally. But it is true that there are many, many more women who are hurt and many more women who come here to exorcists."

To underscore the point, he flipped through his calendar for that particular workweek. Women scheduled for appointments (for both exorcisms and simpler blessings) outnumbered men by about three to one.

Three patients who agreed to be interviewed were

women, including Caterina, the dancer who is working with Father Efrem; Lucia, a housewife; and Francesca, a doctor.

Lucia

The first patient I encountered was Lucia, a forty-four-year-old mother of two from southern Italy. To say "southern Italy" is code for the more backward part of the country, the section that is poorer, underdeveloped, more rural, and less educated; in other words, prone to superstition. (However, several exorcists said they do not see a geographical distribution of possession; while it is true that the south is superstitious, highly sophisticated Milan in the north and nearby Turin, site of the 2006 Winter Olympics, are considered prone to magic and satanic cult activity.)

Like many patients, Lucia was convinced her troubles started when a man who wanted her as a lover but whom she spurned cast an evil spell on her. The year was 1986. She suffered sudden, deep abdominal pains so severe she couldn't walk. She began to lose weight precipitously. Repeated visits to the hospital revealed nothing, relieved nothing. She got sicker and sicker. Doctors finally detected internal bleeding, operated on her, and she slipped into a coma. She remained in the hospital for two months. Once she recovered sufficiently to be discharged, she sought a priest and attended healing masses, including several presided over by Milingo, the African bishop. She only felt worse, often lapsing into a trance during the Mass—a "sign of the presence of the devil," Lucia said. Finally, in 1991, battered, bruised, and disconsolate, she was referred to Father Vincenzo Taraborelli, an exorcist in Rome and protégé of Amorth.

Taraborelli, who describes Lucia as one of his most difficult cases, immediately launched into thrice-a-week meetings with the woman, usually for exorcisms. She would go into a trance, he said, shout vulgarities, rant in languages she didn't know, and struggle so wildly, with such "superhuman strength," that it took the priest and two helpers to hold her down.

At one point, she vomited whole needles, the priest said, another symbol of diabolical torment. "I know people say we are crazy," Lucia's husband, Renzo, said in recounting the ordeal. "You can't believe this stuff until you see it."

Satan "tried to make the impression that Lucia was crazy so that people would think she didn't need a priest but a psychologist," Taraborelli said. "So she tried not to come back [for her sessions with the priest]. Her family had to convince her to return."

Lucia attempted suicide three or four times. She said the devil was making her do things she did not want to do. She was virtually catatonic, languishing at home, paralyzed by inertia, strung out on antidepressants, and unable to work or function socially. She couldn't enter a church without fainting or vomiting, she recalled.

Taraborelli, frustrated, consulted with Amorth. He intensified his prayer sessions with Lucia. Gradually, after twelve years of work, she began to recover and to regain control of herself. She finally felt strong again, able to face problems and, as she put it, "to start to live again."

"There are a lot of priests who do not believe in these things. They think it's all a psychological illness. Especially in America and England, they think it's medieval," Taraborelli said. "And some priests are very scared," he added, recalling the time a twenty-one-year-old woman patient went for his jugular and had to be restrained.

"But when people come to me, I have to let them in." Taraborelli says he sees twenty to thirty people a day who seek blessings and conducts about three or four exorcisms a week, usually with the same handful of people and usually with the more cursory form of exorcism and not the complete ritual. As of mid-2006, he was working with the same six people who return regularly for exorcisms, including two nuns and a seminary student. "When you choose this kind of [religious] life, latent problems come to the forefront to contrast your choice of vocation," he said. Taraborelli works at the Santi Silvestro e Martino ai Monti Church, a ninth-century building flanked by a medieval tower and thought to sit atop the site of one of Rome's very first parish churches.

When I first interviewed Lucia in 2004 for an article in the *Los Angeles Times*, she and her priest said she was cured. She no longer needed exorcisms, but they did continue to pray together regularly. A year later when I sought her out again, Lucia had taken a turn for the worse. She had been committed to a hospital for new illnesses. Her answering machine was broken. She stopped seeing her priest. Ultimately, she dropped from sight.

Taraborelli was worried. When we last spoke, he had not seen Lucia in two months, and someone in her condition needs maintenance, he said. Like a person with an immune deficiency who is vulnerable to disease, a person recovering from demonic influences needs to be surrounded by spiritual reinforcements, prayer, and "the grace of God," the priest said; otherwise the patient is not "armed" against those who would do harm. But all is not lost where Lucia is concerned: Taraborelli believes she had made enough progress so that she is no longer possessed, just "disturbed," and most important, no longer suicidal. A host of other troubles had befallen Lucia: her father had a stroke, her mother suffered a heart attack, and a sister's cancer spread. "Collateral" problems, the priest said, that were interfering with her regular visits to the exorcist, but she continued to pray and will visit when she can.

"She used to suffer just to hear my voice," he said. "Now she can call, we can talk on the phone, she is gentle. It is only after we pray for a while that she gets upset."

One of the most revealing comments in dealing with Lucia came from her husband, Renzo. For all the suffering and horrors, he was grateful that Lucia was possessed and not mentally ill, because the stigma of mental illness would have been too awful to bear. "Thank goodness she's not crazy," Renzo said.

CATERINA

Friday morning—every Friday morning—Caterina spends time with Father Efrem, her priest and exorcist. They pray, then he hears her confession. "The confession gets rid of the material that the evil has caught," Efrem explains. "You want to liberate the soul from obstacles as much as possible before the exorcism." Only then, when necessary, does Caterina undergo an exorcism. "Necessary" is defined by how tormented she is feeling that day and what kind of reactions she exhibits during the prayer. If Efrem sees signs of diabolical interference, he exorcises. And a few hours later, Caterina is back at her routine, which most of the year means teaching dance to dozens of young girls in a Bologna sports hall.

Outside the sports hall, Caterina sprinkles a dash of "holy" salt near the front door. The salt is holy because it has been blessed by Efrem. The sprinkle is for protection.

Inside, the little girls in pink and blue leotards and mini-tutus line up at the dance bar or position themselves on the wooden floor. One long wall of the room is all mirrors; the opposite wall is painted robin's egg blue. Caterina starts with a class of six-year-olds and works up to a final class in which the oldest and most talented aspiring ballerinas are thirteen. It is roughly fifteen hours of instruction, spread over three nights a week. This isn't Juilliard, but it can be grueling nonetheless. The youngest girls are not particularly well-disciplined and some are not particularly graceful. Their arms flail about in a dozen directions; they wobble and giggle. But they are game, and so is Caterina, who remains patient, firm, and steady.

"Come on, little ones," she says with affection at the start of one class. Several of the girls kiss their instructor or hug her after the session ends. She knows their names. Caterina is clothed in black dancing tights and a high-necked, long-sleeved black velour top. Her endless blond hair is tied back in a ponytail with a lavender band. The clothing makes her lithe body seem even longer and sleeker. She wears thick gray socks; there is a small hole in one. She easily glides into dancing positions, through somersaults and rubbery stretches, and from one plié to another. Her back is always ramrod-straight, her posture perfect, her neck extended.

"Flex, point. Flex, point." Again and again. "Up, down. Up, down. Breathe! Breathe!" When they groan at trying to force their bodies into a split, she is strict: "Suffer in silence!" she commands. "You think real dancers don't feel pain? They do! You just don't see it." Among the older girls, there are certainly a few who might make it as accomplished dancers. They sashay diagonally across the floor, revolve in pirouettes, and sweep their arms in circular motions to flawless time and in unerring unison. "Anticipate the moment!" Caterina instructs them. "The Holy Spirit is not going to descend from heaven and give you equilibrium. You have to work at it!" She urges them to "look far away," beyond the walls of the room "to infinity." And later, passionately, "Let's see a little emotion. A little soul. A little heart. A little love."

The mothers and nannies who drop off and pick up the girls are not allowed to stay and watch. Some linger, peeking, or arrive a little before the class is really over. Caterina banishes them; they can be so problematic, she says. "The parents are the worst part. They want me to work miracles," she said. "I'm normally very honest with the children and with their parents about the children's capacity and dancing ability, whether they can ever be professional. I want them to love dance." But parents often don't understand and don't have a very realistic picture of their child's talent. Besides, they can make the child self-conscious watching from the sidelines. Caterina finds meddlesome parents to be the biggest downside of her job. They are annoying, but she prays for them and asks Efrem to include them in his blessings.

In addition to her teaching, Caterina performs on stage in dances and occasionally appears in television entertainment shows. She has lived most of her life in sophisticated Bologna, site of Europe's oldest university, a city that gave the world Copernicus and Petrarch but also served as a center of papal power until the arrival of Napoleon.

No one at her jobs has any inkling of Caterina's spiritual problems. To hear her tell it, and from what I could observe, she does not lapse into uncontrollable or nefarious behavior. "Thank God, it never interfered with my work," she said one night after her classes. We sat at a cozy neighborhood restaurant over plates of ricotta-filled tortelloni. "I know people in the same situation who got fired or who couldn't continue working. The only obstacles I've found are in relationships with people. All my problems have taken away my energy. You can see my work needs lots of energy."

Seeing her in her normal life, it is difficult to understand that this is the same woman who on Friday mornings has the devil driven from her body and soul. Caterina has been through scores, maybe hundreds, of exorcisms. She has been going to Father Efrem weekly since 2000, and before that she consulted Milingo and attended his group pray-alongs. If you think of an exorcism like a therapy session, it may help explain both the restorative power the ritual has over the patient, and his or her dependency on it as well. Caterina says she feels like "a newborn baby" when she emerges from Efrem's weekly care, full of "new energy."

In her big leather handbag, Caterina carries a few indispensable items: the holy salt that she sprinkles where she works and, discreetly, at any other office she has to enter, like a doctor's office or a lawyer's studio; a small plastic bottle of holy water, *acqua benedetta*; and a small canister of baptismal oil. These are for emergencies, should she ever feel an evil spirit coming on. Inside the bag, she also carries a smaller suede zipped pouch that contains pages and pages of prayers, wrapped in plastic with about twenty pictures of Jesus, the Madonna, and various saints.

Caterina also carries the clinical report that a psychologist wrote about her six years ago. It was the third psychologist she had consulted. She didn't care for any of them. They all seemed too intent on blaming the patient, she said, of making the problems that person's responsibility rather than the work of outside forces. She went to each shrink for three or four sessions and then quit.

"They always said it depends on you, on your mentality, the traumas you've had. They always look at the material, not the spiritual. You're crying all the time, and they say what's wrong with you, with your life. They always wanted to give me materialistic explanations, and it stopped there. The more we talked about it, the worse I got. They could not give me an explanation for what was happening." It was a period when she seemed particularly accident-prone; her house burned down, she wrecked the car—incidents she later came to understand were the work of the devil.

With the last psychologist, she submitted to a Minnesota Multiphasic Personality Inventory, a commonly used clinical test for assessing mental health. Three pages with single-spaced typing, folded in fours, and now a little worn. The findings:

Serious emotional disturbance informs all spheres of [patient's] behavior . . . indications of schizophrenia beyond the normal limit . . . elevated quotient of anxiety expressed in psychosomatic forms . . . decisively neurotic. The patient has a clear tendency to fantasize. . . . Tends to be rigid, diffident and susceptible. Sees environment around her as hostile. Suffers personality disturbance, dissociative disturbance, easily mixes up world of fantasy with reality.

Caterina laughs at the diagnosis. "If you believed this, I should be in an insane asylum getting electroshocked," she chuckles. "According to this, I'm schizophrenic." She keeps the report ("a historical document," she calls it) with her so that she can show other troubled souls that they, too, can find spiritual help, as she has, even when the medical establishment has other cures and judgments in mind.

Caterina came to believe she was possessed around 1998. Her adult life to that point had been riddled with immoral behavior, impure thoughts, and drug and alcohol abuse. She came from a family that considered itself Catholic and faithful to God but not one that practiced the religion regularly or formally. She was baptized in church as an infant, but drifted away as she grew older. The Church was not part of her adult life, and instead, she found herself lost spiritually, always in search of answers and a universal truth, but always dissatisfied. In the early nineties, she was living with a boyfriend—a sin in the eyes of the Church, and in Caterina's eyes today as well; priests say people who are not living in a "state of grace" because they are having sex out of wedlock or because they have had an abortion are especially vulnerable to demonic tampering.

Through her boyfriend, Caterina became exposed to tarot cards, fortune-telling, and the occult. Ever looking for something to fill the void in her life, she briefly turned to Buddhism. But she felt increasingly anguished, rudderless, and gripped by terror. She left her boyfriend and moved in with another man, but he was a slave to drugs and alcohol.

"I was a sensitive person. I often felt like I was outside of my body, that my soul had left my body. I was always trying to understand, but it was leading me further from the truth," Caterina said. "I spent a year crying, every day, morning to night, every night. For no reason. Utter anguish. If someone were to tell me that you can die from anguish, I could say I can confirm it."

In 1994, she and her boyfriend finally got help. It started, oddly enough, at a meeting of Alcoholics Anonymous. There, someone told Caterina about liberation masses and she and her boyfriend began attending them eagerly. They would say the rosary every day and attend Mass as frequently as possible. They committed themselves to a life of chastity, ending the sin in their relationship. They helped each other. It was like a "conversion," Caterina says. Around this time, she also attended some of Emmanuel Milingo's services. It was a period when he frequently took his show on the road, holding prayer sessions all over the country. She and her boyfriend saw Milingo in the Veneto region in northern Italy.

The deep anxiety and depression that Caterina was experiencing still did not go away, however. And she was starting to have odd reactions at Mass: she'd faint, feel an overwhelming need to vomit, or lapse into screaming fits; she'd fall from her chair or writhe on the floor. Initially, the idea of demonic possession seemed weird to her, but she kept asking herself, "Why are these bad things happening to me? Why do I feel this way?" Slowly, she came to believe that she needed an exorcist. In part, this was the suggestion of priests she consulted; they saw the violence within her, she said, and told her she should see an exorcist. It was hit-and-miss at first, finding the right sympathetic ear.

"At first, no one believes your story. I went to the first exorcist and he laughed at me. He didn't believe me. And he was an exorcist!" Caterina recalled. "But then he did an exorcism and he realized it was true."

"I was desperate," she added. In time, she embarked on a program of regular exorcisms. "It was the only thing that made me feel better."

Caterina today is not Efrem's only patient, but she is perhaps his most difficult one. He holds counseling sessions for a group every Wednesday night to instruct the

faithful in how to protect themselves against the devil.
Those who attend include housewives with problems at
home, men in their forties, and disturbed youths. He explains that loyal following of the holy sacraments and
prayer are tools of self-defense, like wearing a helmet
against evil.

"We explain not only what the devil is, but tell them
how to become stronger," he said. "We wash the soul like
we wash a body stinking with flies."

To prepare himself for his duties, Efrem rises every
morning at 3:45 and prays for four hours. He has worked
as an exorcist for twelve years, becoming indoctrinated in
a "baptism of fire." He says he has to confess regularly to
keep himself clean. (Catholics believe that confession to
a priest, a central tenet of their faith, is necessary to obtain God's forgiveness for all manner of sins.) It is only in
a clean state that he can fight the devil. "If he sees I have
sins, he knows," Efrem said. "It is the holiness that sends
the devil away."

Efrem says he is able to "feel" the devil during an exorcism, but he cannot quite explain what that feeling is
like. And he feels a lightness at the end of the exorcism as
the devil's grasp weakens. "The devil loses his strength
progressively," he said. "In the beginning he is shouting
and hitting back. Finally, he just sits. He loses his
strength."

Efrem is not sure Caterina will ever be cured.

Caterina is clearly a person whose grasp on reality is
tenuous. She constantly needs to find an explanation for

her problems in causes outside of her control. "Every day," she says woefully, "every day, something happens to me." A bad knee becomes inflamed. She has a car wreck. She loses a job. All of these developments and more she blames on a demonic force that "exaggerates things" and pumps minor troubles into major traumas. Rather than recognize personal responsibility, she sees influences beyond her will.

And so, her answer is a regular program of exorcism with a priest as her accomplice. In the session I witnessed during the summer of 2005, Caterina repeatedly lunged and contorted, her voice went through a number of tones and personalities, and she cursed her priest. Still, said Efrem, Caterina is making progress. She used to be a lot more violent.

But at the end of the session, Caterina looked wilted. The lithe dancer moved stiffly, as if in pain. "I feel very heavy," she said from the green plastic chair. "I feel his presence, like I could touch it, like it's tangible," she said of the devil. "Now it's hard for me to get up. I feel like I'm nailed down." Eventually, she would revive, pick up her bag, and head out the church door.

The first time I met Caterina, before the exorcism, she struck me as an attractive woman who seemed perfectly normal. From appearances, I expected nothing out of the ordinary. We sat in the church, chatted, and she was pleasant, but gradually the details of her sad story unfolded. She said she had come to accept her tribulations because, like Jesus Christ, people must suffer to atone their sins and truly know God. Often she lectures people she meets about Jesus and takes their names to ask her priest to pray for them.

Suddenly, as she was describing this, Caterina went into an abrupt convulsion. Efrem sprang to her side with his cross, looked to the sky, and prayed. She calmed but had lost her voice. She could continue talking only very hoarsely. In a way, this episode, coming out of the blue as it did, was scarier to me than the later exorcism itself. It was completely unexpected and unnerving.

"The devil is present," she croaked. "He doesn't want me to tell you this. He doesn't want you to know."

FRANCESCA

Francesca is a doctor at a small hospital in Italy's eastern Le Marche ("The Marches") region, a lovely, bucolic land-scape facing the Adriatic Sea and sprinkled with hilltop medieval villages. Her life started to fall apart gradu-ally—first unexplained medical ailments, then accidents at work. It became more and more difficult for her to hold things together. She sought doctors, her colleagues, but they found nothing fundamentally wrong. She con-sulted a psychiatrist, an old friend of her father. He couldn't cure her either. Francesca became convinced that her debility was some form of diabolical influence.

Today, Francesca says she has been cured and she is back to work and to a relatively normal life. She was not the victim of a full demonic possession, she says, but rather, had fallen prey to a curse placed on her by a woman who coveted, and eventually obtained, Francesca's one-time fiancé.

To reach her present point of recovery, Francesca first spent a year under the care of Father Francois-Marie Dermine, the exorcist of Ancona. But she decided she was not getting the desired results and turned instead to Bishop Milingo, attending sessions at his compound up to three times a week for nine months. There, she says, she was finally healed. Afterwards she moved to his compound to work for him for nearly two years. She and Milingo became close friends; he even traveled to Francesca's hometown and stayed at the home she shares with her parents. Her mother waited on him, serving him breakfast in bed.

Francesca, thirty-three, is the daughter of a very religious stay-at-home mother and a now-retired father who ran a small business supplying local factories with raw materials for the making of shoes, a regional specialty. She is an only child with a middle-class upbringing and a standard Italian public education. Slightly overweight and with brown hair and large, expressive eyes, Francesca has a hearty, openmouthed laugh and a sense of humor. She can even laugh at aspects of her ordeal. At least, she can now.

What makes her case especially interesting is that her psychiatrist signed off on her seeing an exorcist. He said he could find nothing wrong with her that conformed to medical textbooks, so why not?

Under the Italian educational system, a student can earn a medical degree in four years of what in the United States would be undergraduate university. To specialize, then, the student must study an additional number of years (depending on the field), and following that, he or she will begin working under the supervision of a more experienced doctor. The system may be somewhat less rigorous than preparation for a medical career in the United States, but a doctor is a doctor, a person for whom science and empirical knowledge reign supreme. And yet, even with her education Francesca came to believe that her affliction was supernatural.

After obtaining a medical degree in 1997, Francesca began specializing in urology, a five-year process in the Italian system. To do so, she worked at a hospital in a city near her home, studying under a more senior doctor and practicing under his supervision, an arrangement similar to a hospital internship in the United States.

In October 2000, Francesca traveled with other doctors from the hospital to a conference in Innsbruck, Austria. While there, she woke up one morning and found her right arm was paralyzed. Frightened that she might have had a stroke, she went to a hospital, but doctors there could not determine a specific cause for the paralysis, which eventually subsided. She returned home to Italy and in the following days she noticed numbness in her hands and feet. About a week later, she awoke with a ferocious headache. Turning on a light made her want to throw up. She got worse and worse as the morning wore on. Francesca checked herself into the hospital, but again, doctors could not offer a concrete diagnosis. "They did every possible scan," she said. They told her to go home and rest. She felt better, but a few days later, she was with her fiancé at his veterinary practice when she began bleeding profusely from the genital area. She went back to the hospital, was examined by three gynecologists, and again, there was no explanation, as Francesca remembers it. The doctors sent her home.

Her mother was beginning to fret. She persuaded Francesca to visit a local ninety-three-year-old fortune-teller who was something of a legend in the region for her purported skills to divine the future and read the past. "If you do not go to a priest, you will die," the old woman told Francesca.

Francesca initially resisted the suggestion and continued to consult doctors. "I wasn't one to believe in that stuff," she said, "stuff" like curses and magic and demonic possession. Finally her mother persuaded her to see a priest "for a blessing."

Seeing a priest only aggravated her condition. "I was so bad off that I don't even remember what happened at that first meeting," she said. "My mother told me that the priest was screaming, and I was screaming even louder. Finally, he ordered my mother to take me away from him." He became the first of several priests who refused to work with her. "We would go to one after another and they would all send us away, because they said what I had was too strong." (While Francesca's recollections on this point are her own, it is true that many priests will refuse to attend to parishioners who appear radically disturbed, either out of fear or because they simply do not feel themselves competent to judge what really ails the person.)

Months into her mysterious illness, Francesca's fiancé broke off their engagement. "He left me," she recalled. "He said he did not know why, but he could not be with me." (She later was convinced that it was the spell cast on him and her by the jealous rival who, in fact, ended up with the man.) Soon thereafter came a turning point. Francesca was still working at the hospital where she practiced. One morning she was trying to remove a catheter from a patient. Her hands were trembling. She needed to move the tubing to the left but her hands went to the right. "I had the sensation that my hands were being guided by someone else," Francesca said. She quit the hospital that day.

(It would be three years before Francesca could resume her studies, only after she concluded that she was healed.)

Finally, Francesca found Father Dermine. He was the first priest to receive her and agree to work with her. They met on an almost daily basis for a year. Even as his horrified assistants abandoned the cause, she said, Dermine soldiered on. "Poor thing, he really tried to help," she said. Francesca describes the period as one in which she suffered persistent physical pain; there were times she literally started to bleed when the exorcist placed a crucifix to her body, and many episodes in which she would vomit foam as the priest prayed or offered her Communion. She steadily lost weight, as Dermine continued to incant blessings for the young woman before him.

"He prayed, and prayed, and prayed, and prayed," she said. "He'd even pray before I arrived, because he was afraid I wouldn't arrive."

The more one talks to Francesca, the more bizarre her story becomes. She tells of a visit she made to a charismatic at a convent in San Severino who instructed her to get rid of a gold necklace and ring that her ex-fiancé had given her and who then claimed that items in her house, including her mattress and pillow, were cursed. She complied, ridding herself of the jewelry and cleansing her home of its cursed furnishings. Francesca's matter-of-fact descriptions of these actions is all the more disconcerting coming from a woman of science, a woman who practiced, even on a junior scale, medicine.

As time went on, Francesca came to believe that Father Dermine was not helping her. Her desperate condition was only getting worse; she had no progress to report. Increasingly, she thought of death, of suicide, as the only way out. She came close to hurling herself out the upper-story window of her home. She was convinced that satanic cults had her in their sights, and that her tremors, malaise, nausea, and blinding headaches intensified when they were invoking incantations against her.

The nights were the absolute worst times, when she could not sleep, lay feverishly awake, and believed she saw satanic worshippers chanting ritually around candles, or heard the doors and windows in her home open and close by themselves. Prodded by her deeply pious mother, Francesca finally decided to seek out Milingo, whose flamboyance made him seem like a "quick-fix" exorcist compared to the more methodical, careful, and according to Francesca, less effective Dermine.

On January 9, 2003, Francesca had her first appointment with Milingo. She and her parents arrived at his compound in Zagarolo and sat through the regular Mass inside the large white tent. Francesca cried throughout the service and dreaded meeting the famous African prelate. When the Mass concluded, there was a long line of people waiting to be received by Milingo. Because she had an appointment, thanks to a friendly priest who intervened on her behalf, Francesca was whisked to the front of the line and quickly found herself seated before the man about whom she had heard so much.

"I cried a lot," she said. "I told him I had been to many priests, that I had been told that someone had cast a spell on me and wants me dead. He just let me talk." He prayed, then rose to his feet and prayed some more. Within minutes, Francesca felt robbed of all strength and she began to gag. "Leave her in peace!" Milingo called out, to no one visible. "She is not your daughter! She is a daughter of God!" Slowly, Francesca found herself regaining control of herself, of a presence of mind.

"From today, you will start a new life," Milingo told Francesca.

"Am I healed?" she asked as she started to recover.

"Absolutely not," he responded, as Francesca recalled later. "But we will make sure it will happen. It will, however, take time."

He also immediately forced her to choose between him and Dermine. She could not see both, he said. She chose Milingo.

On the long drive home from Zagarolo, Francesca fell into a deep sleep. She slept until the next day, peacefully, for the first time in years. Her hands stopped trembling. "I will never forget it."

The treatment with Milingo over the next nine months required many sacrifices, Francesca said. At first she traveled to his compound once a week, and later three times a week—a four-hour drive—for personal sessions with Milingo. At one point, he locked her in a room with a picture of Jesus, a gesture he told her would help cure her. Francesca said she cried and cried for hours, beating the door and demanding to be released.

Around September of that year, Milingo pronounced her cured, that the spell that had cursed her was "dissolved." Francesca, indeed, felt cured. The headaches and insomnia were gone. She was once again in control of her thoughts and actions. He then asked her to move into the compound where the bishop and his coterie of nuns lived and to work for him. She readily agreed and took on tasks that included keeping his appointment schedule and managing the accounting of proceeds coming into the compound gift shop. She traveled to Africa with him and helped him write some of his books. She was the only layperson and the only non-African living in the shared Zagarolo house.

Certainly there were tensions and, it appears, resentment and adjustment. The restrictions of life at the compound were completely new for Francesca. The only child suddenly found herself surrounded by "brothers and sisters," sleeping in cramped quarters, waiting for the bathroom, and sharing the dinner table with a crowd. One could not turn on the television set without permission of the mother superior, for example, and all women were expected to dress in a particularly modest fashion. The African nuns wore long skirts, made of brightly colored fabric with geometric designs, and their hair was swept up in headscarves; they also wore long sleeves and high collars. The nuns were constantly rebuking Francesca for not obeying the rules, yet she clearly remained a favorite of Milingo. "I frequently asked him, 'Why me?' He had healed so many. But he never gave me an answer."

In the summer of 2005, nearly two years after she began living at the compound, Francesca decided it was time to move on. She returned home to live with her parents. Milingo followed, in need of medical treatment for a bum knee, treatment that he sought at a hospital near Francesca's hometown. He spent several weeks of recovery living in an upstairs bedroom at Francesca's family home. Her parents fed him, providing any food he requested; when he wanted ice cream, he got ice cream. Milingo called her parents "Mamma and Papà," Francesca said. "He feels at home with us."

Today, Francesca has achieved some distance from Milingo. In part, it appears she feels the need to stand on her own two feet. She returned to her studies and her urology internship at the hospital, where she says her superiors only know that she was ill, had to go away, and is now recovered.

"I am a changed person. Everyone in my family is changed," she said. "I used to go to church only on Sundays. Now I pray every day. Sometimes for hours."

Francesca said that Father Dermine had told her to pray for the woman whom she believes cursed her. She needed to forgive the woman to become healed, he told her. But every time she prayed for the woman, Francesca became nauseous. Milingo had a different approach. Don't even think about her, he said. At the end of her time with Milingo, Francesca said she no longer harbored anger or ill will toward the woman whom she believes ruined her life.

Although it cannot be verified, this is what Francesca believes: The woman, a rival for the affections of Francesca's then-fiancé, consulted a magician who helped her put a curse on Francesca. The woman eventually called Francesca and threatened her life. The devil acts through magicians, tarot cards, pendulums, and other accoutrements of the underworld.

"You used to hear about this kind of stuff, but it seems very far off until it happens to you," Francesca said. "I didn't believe it. But in the face of certain occurrences, we can only lift our hands and accept it. The devil's strength is that people don't believe in him. That was my problem. I didn't believe."

Francesca's psychiatrist didn't believe either, and he still doesn't. But he decided that an exorcist was the best therapy for his patient.

Dr. Pier Domenico Ruggieri, sixty-two, had known Francesca since she was a little girl. A longtime family friend, he was the psychiatrist that Francesca and her parents turned to when her unexplained troubles became acute. Ruggieri has been practicing psychiatry for nearly forty years and was head of the department of psychology at the hospital in Macerata, one of the largest towns in Le Marche, until retiring from that position in 2002. Confronted with this puzzling case, Ruggieri examined Francesca and, he said, attempted to treat her symptoms, including what he determined were depression and anxiety. But her overall condition, the symptoms she displayed and the experiences she described, taken together, defied categorization.

He continued to see her and remained stumped. He could not diagnose a specific mental illness. Around this time, Francesca, at the end of her rope, began seeing Milingo. Ruggieri knew of the African bishop by reputation, which was not a particularly good one, in his opinion. He remembered seeing a bizarre ritual that Milingo presided over years earlier in which thousands of people gathered and became swept up in a kind of mass hysteria. People screamed, hurled themselves on the ground, and ripped away their clothes. It was an "infernal snake pit," the doctor recalled. Deeply skeptical, Ruggieri eventually met Milingo in person, and his opinion shifted. Most important, Ruggieri says, he noted improvement in Francesca as soon as she began to see Milingo. "From the moment she went to Milingo, she changed totally. She gained her equilibrium. She regained herself." The exorcist was doing something right, Ruggieri concluded.

"I am a layperson," said Ruggieri, describing himself as a believer in God who reserves doubts about many aspects of formal religion. "Science forbids us from even thinking of these things. I certainly don't believe in magic spells. I would not like to believe in demonic possession.

"But I see things that make me think. There are facts that you have to consider and that you cannot hide behind scientific blame. You cannot always explain everything with psychological analysis. To explain some things out of the ordinary, normal scientific parameters are not enough."

Ruggieri's private practice is located above the pharmacy in Macerata on a narrow winding street. The office is decorated in blue: the furniture, the carpet, the filing cabinets—everything is blue. Thick textbooks on topics such as "Depressive Disturbances" are stacked on his desk, next to sample boxes of psychotherapeutic drugs and antidepressants like Sereupin.

His erstwhile skepticism has been replaced with what he calls "having an open mind." There were several factors that brought Ruggieri around to accepting a "spiritual solution" in Francesca's case. First was his impotence to render a clear medical diagnosis. Second, Francesca was convincingly lucid in describing what was happening to her, and neither she nor her parents seemed eager to attribute her affliction to supernatural causes; they seemed realistic, if baffled, in their assessment of the situation. And finally, he was impressed by Milingo, who he believes may have some higher "primordial" power. He acknowledges that someone with a serious psychosis who is sent to an exorcist risks deeper, harmful, mental trauma. "The thing I appreciate about Milingo is that he is aware of the dangers. He asks us, 'Is there a danger?' Some exorcists don't even bother," Ruggieri said.

And so, Ruggieri the psychiatrist has sent five or six patients—those for whom he can find no concrete explanation for their symptoms—to Milingo the exorcist.

CHAPTER VI

Satanic Cults

They called themselves the Beasts of Satan, and their sickening crimes stand out as the most extreme case in Italy of homicidal devil worship. Priests can debate whether Satan had anything to do with the crimes; the members of the gang claimed to have made a pact with the devil, and exorcists point to such cases as evidence of concrete, activist evil in the world. As far as police and prosecutors were concerned, however, the Beasts were driven by drugs and a craven disregard for humanity.

To be sure, the murders outside Milan, in northern Italy, shocked the nation. Newspapers and television talk shows were full of lurid headlines and graphic descriptions. The gang—part sect, part amateur rock band—was said to have a penchant for nefarious ceremonies, violent sex, black candles, snakes, the skulls of goats, and the number 666; in other words, all the trappings of satanic cults. In 2005, Andrea Volpe, a man in his early twenties when the killings began, and seven accomplices were condemned in a court of law to long prison sentences for their roles in the murder of three friends and for forcing the suicide of a fourth who attempted to escape the sect. According to testimony and a chilling diary that Volpe kept, which was leaked in part to the Italian press, the first victims of the Beasts of Satan were killed in 1998. They were sixteen-year-old Fabio Tollis and nineteen-year-old Chiara Marino. Both had belonged to the Beasts of Satan, and Tollis was lead singer in the gang's heavy-metal band. Marino, the convicted killers later claimed, had come to personify in their warped minds the Virgin Mary and had to die; Tollis was killed when he resisted the deadly plot.

Under a full moon on a winter night in the woods just north of Milan, Volpe and his accomplices used a knife to kill Marino, plunging the blade into her heart. They then took a hammer and pummeled Tollis to death. The murders were carried out as part of a long, grisly ordeal described by investigators as a ritualistic human sacrifice. The two were buried in a six-foot-deep pit, dug there under the trees. After chucking the lifeless pair into the ground, the convicted killers later testified, they urinated on the bodies. One of the group smoked cigarettes and threw the butts into the grave. As far as their families or anyone else knew, Marino and Tollis simply disappeared.

Six years later, in 2004, the Beasts were at it again. Volpe and his girlfriend, Elisabetta Ballarin, lured one of Volpe's former girlfriends, Mariangela Pezzotta, twenty-seven, to a remote chalet outside Milan for a drug-fueled party. Pezzotta was reportedly threatening to make the earlier murders public. She had to go. The three ate dinner and shared a toast of champagne. Then Volpe shot her in the face and buried her, alive, in a shallow grave. Another accomplice later arrived and finished her off with a shovel.

Only when that murder was discovered, and police arrested Volpe, did the first slayings come to light. In a bid for leniency, Volpe agreed to cooperate with investigators. He led a team that included police and forensic archaeologists to the deep hole where Tollis and Marino lay. Their bones were excavated, along with the knife, bits of a broken spade, cloth, and leather. Investigators were able to reconstruct the bodies and pinpoint the many wounds in the bones. Volpe, the only participant who admitted to the deeds in court, was sentenced to thirty years in prison. The crimes had "a level of cruelty and savagery . . . that I have never seen before in my career," lead prosecutor Antonio Pizzi, a veteran with more than three decades of experience, told the Reuters news agency when the sect members went on trial.

Police found Volpe's diary in a bag with human hair

and teeth—decorations, apparently, for black masses. In the diary, Volpe spelled it out:

> We are wicked individuals. We plague the people and we play with their lives.
> We know no pity.
> Pitiless, we will eliminate and cleanse, donating the ash of our enemies to he who sits on the throne.

† † †

For many Italians the Beasts of Satan case confirmed their worst nightmare, the very thing that many of their priests warned them about. It exemplified the purported growth of satanic cults in Italy, proof that a troubled, amoral generation of young people, gullible, lost, and desperate, is turning away from God and toward the occult, pseudo-witchcraft, and in the extreme, devil worship. Church officials blame the trend, in part, on the alienation of today's youth, the breakdown of the family, and the explosion of satanic-related material available on the Internet and in popular, egoistic, and self-absorbed culture.

The spheres of the exorcist and the satanic cult do not intersect directly. Members of cults rarely, if ever, seek out an exorcist. And the exorcists maintain that the patients they work with are people whose "possession" or disturbance is not the result of an overt petition to evil, with the exception of only the most casual of dabbling in the occult, such as seeing a fortune-teller or holding a séance. Devil worshippers have made a far more conscious, extreme, and malevolent choice. Yet the study of cults is relevant to exorcists because they are convinced that the existence of cults and of pop-Satanism feeds an unhealthy climate that spreads evil.

For fundamentalists like Father Amorth, who sees the devil around every corner, the Beasts case confirms their worldview and constitutes further proof of Satan as a real force whose presence is undeniable. And quite a few patients become convinced (whether their affliction is real or a figment of their imagination) that they have been cursed by a cult member who, for whatever reason, has targeted them. They imagine their names being chanted in satanic rituals or spells cast over their photographs. When they hear of stories like the Beasts of Satan, they, and other susceptible people like them, become more convinced of the risks lurking close at hand. Priests argue that youths are especially vulnerable.

"There is a growing interest in satanic cults among youth today," said Carlo Climati, an instructor at a pontifical university in Rome who specializes in youth alienation issues. "They hear it in music, they find it on the Internet. Ten years ago when young people wanted to find out about Satanism, it was difficult. Now it's very easy."

All of the prosecuted Beasts of Satan were under the age of thirty when the killings took place; several were in their teens and one was a minor. Sociologists say that Milan, Italy's sophisticated financial and fashion capital, and other sections of northern Italy are home to more disaffected youth than southern Italy, in part because the family structure in the north is weaker. As Italian cities go, Milan more closely resembles its counterparts elsewhere in Europe, complete with an urban core, housing projects, intense work pressures, and presumably, more fertile ground for alienation and loneliness.

Experts caution, however, that the phenomenon can easily be exaggerated. The fears are out of proportion to the actual danger, according to several academics and law enforcement officials. The Beasts of Satan case is the only confirmed incident of murder by devil worshippers in Italy in at least several decades, authorities say. Massimo Introvigne, the expert on alternative religions, estimates that there are today perhaps several hundred satanic sects in Italy, encompassing only four to five thousand people. The respected Italian research institute Eurispes said a couple of years ago that it had identified 650 satanic organizations in Italy, most of them in the northern Lombardy region that includes Milan.[1] Some are very much above ground, publishing magazines and managing active Web sites; several are even legally incorporated. Few of these groups commit serious crimes, Introvigne says. It's the wannabes who "don't know where to stop," are not organized, and are usually societal dropouts and deviants with little to lose who pose the more serious threat in their eagerness to emulate the satanically inspired. Even among those, most of the crimes they commit involve drug dealing and vandalism, not the worst of possible felonies.

Introvigne does not include the case of a popular nun and headmistress at a religious boarding school who was murdered by three girls, ages sixteen and seventeen, in the affluent northern town of Chiavenna in the summer of 2000. The girls lured sixty-year-old Sister Maria Laura Mainetti into an ambush and stabbed her numerous times, authorities said. Although news reports at the time said the girls' diaries contained satanic symbols and tributes to death-rock singer Marilyn Manson, and that one of the girls confessed to wanting the nun's body to "sacrifice" in a "game," there was no evidence that the girls belonged to a sect.

Introvigne also does not include the Satan's Children case from Bologna that so disturbed Father Dermine because no charges ever stuck. "We never had a real scare," Introvigne said. However, that does not mean there is no cause for alarm. In fact, the number of hard-core, mostly juvenile offenders remains consistent and suggests, in Introvigne's opinion, that there will be periodic incidents like the Beasts of Satan in the future. "I am concerned that there will be crucial incidents, but it is important not to overreact. Inflating the problem does not help."

† † †

Aldo Buonaiuto is a young priest who specializes in the counseling and rehabilitation of what he says are young Italians who become ensnared by satanic sects. These are primarily victims who are unwittingly brought into a cult ceremony where they might be drugged, raped, or otherwise abused. Buonaiuto got into this business through his initial ministry, which involved rescuing prostitutes from the streets, giving them shelter, and helping them find legitimate jobs. He began to hear more and more scary tales of cult activity and saw the need for his help. Buonaiuto speaks in measured tones and is not given to hyperbole—he thinks, for example, that the use of exorcism has become unnecessarily and perilously excessive—but he would certainly beg to differ from the academics and others who minimize the problem of satanic sects.

"This is not an isolated phenomenon," he said. The priest clarifies that many of the so-called sects are not really into devil worship per se; they use the trappings perhaps, such as drawing pentagrams on the ground or burning candles around an inverted crucifix. Mostly, they are groups of no-goodniks who consume hard drugs, engage in orgies, and attempt to pull in other corrupt souls whom they can psychologically "imprison." They should be seen more as a criminal organization than an alternative system of religious belief.

Buonaiuto, who lives in a house behind high walls in a small town near Ancona, operates a twenty-four-hour telephone hotline for people who think they have been harmed by sects or who suspect a loved one might have been hurt or might have joined one. A five-member team staffs the hotline and receives an average of eight to ten calls a day from all over the country. Some are bogus, threats, and vulgarities, but many are legitimate appeals for help, often from people who have had a hard time finding someone who takes them seriously, according to Buonaiuto, whose name translates as "good help."

"I listen to them a lot and make them feel we believe in them. Whether it's true or not, they are a victim, and that's the first thing," he said. "Many people are terrorized. Most have already been unbelieved elsewhere." Judging by the nature and severity of the complaint, he attempts to meet with the callers and eventually encourages them to go to the police or to seek medical or psychiatric help if that seems more appropriate.

In one call that Buonaiuto tape-recorded, a man in his twenties described going to a party with his girlfriend, a party that they had heard about but where they did not know anyone. Some of those in attendance launched into a strange form of prayer, and the man and his girlfriend attempted to leave but found the doors locked. He then passed out, having consumed only a Coke, which he later realized must have been spiked. When he woke up hours later, just before dawn, he found his girlfriend unconscious and nude, with signs that she had been raped. They went to a hospital but have been too traumatized to report the incident to the authorities.

Buonaiuto is also in contact with one of the Beasts of

Satan. Pietro Guerrieri was sentenced to sixteen years in jail for his role in the murders. He did not directly participate in the killing but dug the pit where the first young victims, Tollis and Marino, were buried. After his conviction, Guerrieri asked to see a priest, saying he wanted therapy. Buonaiuto and Guerrieri have been meeting about once a month and exchanging letters. Wary at first about Guerrieri's motives, the priest now says he is surprised at the large degree of compassion he finds himself feeling for the man, who is now twenty-five.

Buonaiuto has come to see Guerrieri more as a victim than a leader, an instrument manipulated by evil people. His troubled background, Buonaiuto thinks, is typical of fragile youths who get sucked into violent counterculture lifestyles. Guerrieri's parents were divorced and remarried; his mother was mentally ill and his father distant. A younger brother was killed in a car accident. He started snorting cocaine and shooting up heroin when he was sixteen and opened a tattoo parlor when he was eighteen. He first met the Beasts when they came in to have pentagrams and other symbols tattooed on their bodies.

Initially he didn't take seriously their bizarre talk of human sacrifice, love for Satan, and hatred for almost everyone else. But he went along with them to drop acid and hang out at heavy-metal nightclubs, where he watched the others descend into hazy, mumbling trances, or bounce off the walls in rage-filled explosions. He also went along with them on strange forays into the forest, where they would stand on the points of a star, clutching the photograph of a perceived enemy, and pronounce a spell that would certainly bring harm to the target of their wrath. Eventually Guerrieri became convinced that his associates were indeed quite capable of murder and he wanted out. But he was equally convinced they would kill him if he tried to leave. It was only after Tollis and Marino were slain that he mustered the courage to drop out of the Beasts, though he continued to live in fear, always looking over his shoulder, until his arrest in 2004. Guerrieri appears to be the only member of the sect who has shown remorse for the crimes and, according to Buonaiuto, he is the only one to pay reparations to the families of the two victims. He is in a maximum-security jail for his own protection.[2]

"If someone does something evil, it has to come from somewhere," Father Buonaiuto said. "For me, the devil is something more indirect than direct, a negative principle. In these cases, I think there is always something evil in the person's background, or in the family, or in the society around him."

In that, Buonaiuto differs from the exorcists (even though they call upon him on occasion for his expert advice) because he finds causes beyond a personified Satan to explain such evil. Despite the depravity of cases like the Beasts of Satan, the exorcists will not find a whole lot of support in law enforcement circles either.

† † †

A study prepared by the Italian police for the 2005 International Congress on Law and Mental Health, held in Paris, emphasized the need to view the criminal behavior of so-called satanic sects through the same prism used to evaluate common criminals—that is, free of the "symbolic wrapping" of other-worldly, esoteric mystery "created on purpose to better commit various crimes."[3]

From a purely law enforcement perspective, the greater concern is sects that persuade members to relinquish their wealth and assets to the larger group (and, usually, to the pockets of the two or three main leaders), or that persuade members to do other favors, sexual or otherwise.

Police commander Marco Strano, a co-author of the study and one of Italy's leading law enforcement experts on cults, helped found an "anti-sect" unit that, like Buonaiuto's operation, receives emergency calls every day. Most of the legitimate callers request intervention to rescue a relative who has abandoned the family to join a cult. While this kind of activity is old hat in the United States, it is relatively new in Italy.

Until a few years ago, Satanists favored an abandoned mental asylum on the outskirts of Rome, where police periodically found the remains of sacrificed small animals like cats and graffiti espousing devil worship. But that has subsided, Strano said; young people still use the asylum but most adult (and more serious) Satanists prefer private houses and more discreet venues. Strano believes Catholic priests have overstated the threat of satanic cults, which he, like Introvigne and others, says have committed only a limited number of major crimes and have seen their influence plateau. Strano is a tall, thin man given to those very Italian haughty shrugs, accompanied by a dramatic raising of a thick black eyebrow. He is skeptical, even dismissive, of the alarm bells that the Church has sounded. The vast majority of adults who seek out the occult and the cults do so of their own free will, he said, enticed by the excitement and adventure.

"Priests have difficulty admitting that people go to cults independently," he said. "For the priests, it's competition."

The danger, in Strano's view, comes from the breakdown of society when today's youthful Satanists become adults. This occurs not because of religious disaffection but because of their alienation from the normal workings of modern interaction. Religion, he stressed, is not the major concern. Strano adamantly insists on interpreting the phenomenon of Satanism from a purely secular, nonreligious perspective, one of "empirical science" in which criminals are criminals, and little else matters. As a secular institution, he pointed out, the state police has little time for the fears of priests, and instead treats the cult phenomenon as a law enforcement issue.

I interviewed Strano in a state police headquarters inside a nineteenth-century French-built fortress in northeastern Rome. As we walked outside to the street to await my taxi, we passed the chapel. A chapel? In a secular institution like the state police? "We have Mass every

Friday morning," Strano said. "If we do not attend, the priest scolds us." So much for the secular institution, I said to Strano. At that point, he pulled from under his collar a thick wooden cross, a gift from the priest who was concerned about Strano's line of work and usual clientele. This man of empirical science in this secular institution was clearly not taking any chances.

"Even we men of empirical science have moments of weakness," he said.

CHAPTER VII

Divergence Within the Church

A snapshot of the ambivalence of the Church toward demonic possession and exorcism can be seen in the foreword Father Benedict J. Groeschel wrote to the English-language translation of Father Amorth's first book.[1] As one reviewer put it, it was one of the most tepid endorsements known to the publishing world. A foreword normally tells people to read the book; Groeschel, a Franciscan priest with a doctorate in psychology from Columbia University, opens by admitting that he initially declined the request to write the foreword: "Although I have had experience with those suffering from what I am convinced were diabolical influences, I have difficulties with Father Amorth's approach."

Groeschel, based in New York, developed a reputation over the years as one of American Catholicism's top experts in paranormal behavior and demonic influence. Yet, he told American author Michael W. Cuneo in 1996, in all the cases that were sent his way, he never discerned what he believed was a true case of demonic possession. (He differentiates "demonic oppression," which is less serious than possession and can be cured with prayers but does not require a full exorcism; he did encounter these cases, he said.)[2]

Groeschel finally recommends Amorth's book by, essentially, suspending his academic credentials. "As a priest rather than a clinician, I recognize in this book the account of an intelligent and dedicated pastor of souls who has had the courage to go where most of us fear to tread." Amorth "makes us think," he adds. "This book needs to be read with care but with an open mind."

The Vatican openly and publicly endorses the work of exorcists, as witnessed in Pope Benedict XVI's recent blessing, but it frowns on the proliferation of healing masses and an overwrought, exaggerated emphasis on exorcism. It does not want the ritual to become the focus of massive public revelry. It prefers a more discreet approach, that exorcists and their work not be publicized so as not to encourage it or focus unwanted attention on it. It also does not want exorcists sucked into a "kind of trip," as one official put it. The Congregation for Divine Worship, which oversaw the exorcism guidelines drawn up in 1999, has asked bishops not to publish the names of their exorcists, and some dioceses in the United States—Los Angeles is one of them—will not release the names. But the rules are applied with less rigidity in Italy, although few exorcists are as keen on grabbing headlines as Amorth.

The Congregation for Divine Worship disapproves of Amorth, according to a senior official there. Publicity around exorcism "is more damaging than helpful," the official said. He expressed doubt that Amorth performs exorcisms with the frequency that he claims, and said the "highly unlikely" scenario of exorcising all day long "loses all sense of perspective and balance." Still, the Vatican has not tried to shut Amorth down. Generally, the top Church hierarchy defers to the bishops, who are meant to enforce restrictions and decorum and report problems to the Vatican only when they, the bishops, need assistance. The official said the Congregation steps in occasionally, but the impression I got is that it would practically take something as egregious as an exorcist going on *Oprah* before it would crack down. Or a case like Milingo, of course, or a situation of death or drastic abuse. That explains why exorcists can tailor their practice, within certain broad outlines, and seem at times to be following their own rules.

The Congregation will accept petitions from exorcists

who reject the revised rite and wish to continue using the old one; generally the Congregation will grant permission. It has steadfastly refused, however, to give any formal recognition to the International Association of Exorcists founded by Amorth because of uncertainty over who all the members are and what their agendas are.

"This is the sort of thing that brings with it exhilaration and gets into people's heads," the official said. "There is a certain hysteria among priests, too. Some of this is self-perpetuated. It makes you wonder if the psyche is not in control."

The official requested anonymity because he was not authorized to criticize a fellow priest publicly.

Too many exorcists, Amorth among them, tend to see the devil everywhere, from horoscopes and Ouija boards to yoga and Harry Potter. And there is an internal contradiction in a fundamental aspect of their thinking: priests blame superstition for fomenting the problem by leading people away from God, yet they also validate superstition by lending credence to diabolical possession and other supernatural workings of evil forces.

Priests who are less enamored of the exorcism rite point to the cultural conditioning of Italians (and, yes, the Church has a role in it), which promotes belief in the supernatural and miracles and devotion to saints. "We have a culture that is very devotionalist," said Father Aldo Buonaiuto. "In some places, you have a problem, you go immediately to the exorcist. Straight to the exorcist! This is a very negative thing."

Certain movements in the Church contribute to this, although the point of Vatican II was to give reason to faith, Buonaiuto noted. The Second Vatican Council was the wide-ranging reexamination of Church practices in the mid-1960s that led to numerous, more progressive reforms. Among the changes, it became permissible for priests to say Mass in languages other than Latin and to face the congregation instead of maintaining their backs to the audience as had been the practice. Fundamentalists reject many of the changes, and to this day top Church leaders debate the meaning of the reform process. But indisputably it was part of an evolution that has welcomed reason into the faith, and consequently made exorcisms less relevant.

The ambiguity is tied to several debates. Is evil personal or impersonal? An active or passive force? Is the devil real or symbolic? That evil exists in the world is unquestionable. The extent to which evil is the result of bad choices by human beings or the work of a greater intelligent force is where good people may part ways. And if evil is the interplay of something beyond individual dysfunction, where does temptation come from? Where does the suggestion of evil come from? Although the devil sort of fell out of fashion after the Age of Reason, and again after Vatican II, the Church under Pope John Paul II taught that the devil was a real and dangerous presence in society (encouraged by the fact that the Prince of Darkness was very much enshrined in popular Italian culture). For believers, in a world where concrete proof of the existence of God or Satan is hard to come by, exorcism may serve as rare evidence of something otherwise elusive; it reinforces the belief in God that believers want to believe.

Father Gerald O'Collins, the Jesuit theologian, points to the Lord's Prayer, Christianity's seminal deliverance prayer. It ends with the words, "Deliver us from evil." But, O'Collins notes, in its original Greek form, the line was, "Deliver us from the Evil One." The Church over the years changed the specific "Evil One" to a more generic and vague "evil" to tone down the concept. As noted earlier, O'Collins, who is one of Rome's most respected theologians, opposes the facile use of exorcism and believes it should generally be avoided.

"I never met anybody who I thought was possessed. I have met lots of people who were not free, slaves to false idols . . . to drugs, pornography, false standards of society. Imprisoned," he said. "A healthy Church is teaching the word of God. Not going around exorcising demons."

Father Norman Tanner, the Church historian, agrees. "You have only to look at the horrors of the world to know the reality of evil. Or is it our choice? Are we choosing evil? Or is part of evil design a work by the devil? There are the more biblical fundamentalists who want a more literal interpretation. It is not an issue that is easy to get one's hands on. It is not as if there is a clear distinction between personal and impersonal evil. For most people it is an abstract issue."

Exorcism, he said, does not, and it should not, form part of the normal ministry of most priests.

CHAPTER VIII

Skeptics and Shrinks

The capacity of some people to believe the patently unbelievable is limitless. And the capacity of the human mind to fool itself is also limitless. The human mind can allow or cause things to happen while remaining, at least consciously, unaware of them.

Most—but not all—psychiatrists, psychologists, and other scientists dismiss demonic possession as a case of suggestible people acting on subconscious impulses or following the cues of a priest. Indeed, many of the symptoms and behaviors that present themselves during exorcisms and during meetings between priests and patients seeking exorcisms can be explained by science and medical analysis. Many symptoms and behaviors fit the patterns of a litany of known psychological disorders, especially dissociation, schizophrenia, manic depression, and hysteria, or even physiological conditions such as epilepsy and Tourette's syndrome. Some severe forms of epilepsy are accompanied by delirium and hallucinations.

Catholics who think they are possessed tend to seek out a priest over a psychiatrist because a priest will be more predisposed to reinforcing their feelings of spiritual ill-being. A psychiatrist, on the other hand, would force such people to face inner tensions and anxieties and confront true illness.

Many critics think the exorcism ritual itself constitutes a form of hypnosis, creating the same state of consciousness that hypnosis would. The rhythmic incantations of the priest, the patient's inward focus, the isolation—all can submerge a patient into a trance, a hypnotic-like state that allows subconscious role-playing. A kind of emotional contagion sets in that signals certain behavior to the patient. A good hypnotist can make a patient bark like a dog. An exorcist, less explicitly and unintentionally, could make a patient talk like the devil. The phenomenon, say the critics, is compounded by a group setting (a superstitious, religious milieu) that encourages belief in possession and favors external causes for illness and malady over internal possibilities. It is compounded by the preponderance of relatively poor medical care and the stigma attached to psychiatric therapy. Looking for a priest allows a patient to deny his or her illness, which may be more socially palatable.

Psychiatrists define possession as "the delirious

conviction of being possessed by another being—a demon or an animal—which controls gestures, words and thoughts."[1] Demons go from their "exogenous" position in religion to an "endogenous" state, the product of a person's fears, conflicts, and psychological imbalance.[2]

In 2006 the annual congress of the Italian Society of Psychopathology filled two entire floors of one of Rome's fanciest hotels, with thousands of participants—psychiatrists, psychologists, therapists, and other doctors—from all over the country and beyond. The world's largest pharmaceutical firms had booths to hawk their pills for anxiety, depression, and schizophrenia. The latest studies on new finds in the treatment of bipolar depression and a multitude of other conditions were available in glossy pamphlets. And in one wing of the conference, an entire afternoon was dedicated to lectures on "presumed demonic possession," satanic sects, and related topics. One of the lectures was entitled "Exorcism versus Therapy." The turnout for the session was so large that organizers had to relocate everyone to an auditorium three times the size of the original venue.

One of the papers presented at the congress states:

> The cases of presumed demonic possession
> represent a reality that is increasingly being
> reported in mass media, although often with
> little scientific or critical analysis, that makes
> us aware of numerous cases of presumed
> possessed people, Satanic sects and many

other facts related to a belief in the existence of demons, beliefs that are as alive today as in times gone by. The way that cases of presumed possession manifest themselves has remained, in fact, invariable through the course of human history, and so it is possible today to observe this phenomenon in a manner not unlike the manner in which it was observed in medieval times and in the early days of civilization.

Dr. Vincenzo Mastronardi, an expert in psychological pathology at the University of Rome, co-authored that paper and was a keynote speaker at the conference. The phenomenon, he says, has become a vicious circle, of sick or disturbed people wanting to believe in the devil and priests who encourage them. Mastronardi describes himself as a believer and a Catholic, and the nephew of a monsignor, but he said exorcisms are riddled with auto-suggestion, manipulation, and misdiagnosis. They are not always harmful, he hastened to add, but certainly not the preferred treatment.

"From what I have observed in thirty-five years as a clinical psychologist, exorcism is really a kind of hypnosis. It is both autohypnosis and hypnosis by a priest who does it without knowing. And then they think that what happens is the action of the devil. When it ceases, the devil has gone away," Mastronardi said. "Exorcism activities are truly hypnosis sessions. The exorcist priest is not conscious of the fact that he is hypnotizing [the patient] but in reality we know that what happens is a strong will of personal affirmation of that priest, and therefore a vicious circle of auto-influence."

Most typically a person who thinks he is possessed is suffering from a form of what used to be known as hysteria, Mastronardi said. Such a patient is impressionable, easily influenced by other people, films, or séances. He seeks out a priest because the priest will likely confirm the demonic origins of his disease. Exorcists allow the patient's family to be present (in contrast to most psychiatric sessions, which do not), so the patient retains his social unit and gets the attention of his family. "Also," said Mastronardi, "one should not underestimate the behavior of the priest, which is characterized by humanity and empathy, freely expressed by physical contact, hugs, stroking, affectionate gestures, placing of hands, etc. (something which is avidly sought after by these patients). This is something that a therapist can't do because of his role."

Maurizio de Vanna, a psychiatrist from the University of Trieste, has interviewed numerous exorcists, especially in the Trieste region of northern Italy. He notes that the trance induced by the exorcist is different from the state of consciousness attained in a traditional hypnosis. In the exorcism trance, the subject is able to retain the faculties normally available to him or her.

Dissociation is one of the most commonly cited scientific explanations of what is happening in the brain to make a person think he or she is possessed. Dissociation is defined as the compartmentalization of brain processes that are normally integrated. In other words, it is a condition that happens when parts of the brain are not talking to each other, or more important, not talking to the main conscious, "self-aware" part of the brain; then, those parts trigger autonomous behavior that the person is not aware of or doesn't consciously expect. If that behavior is especially out of character, or in any way vile, the person is eager to blame it on malevolent external forces. Society at large, a very religious family, or a superstitious village might reinforce that conclusion. Typically, a person in the early stages of a schizophrenic illness will attempt to explain, justify, or rationalize his problems in a context and through ideas that are acceptable to his social group.[3]

What causes those parts of the brain to act on their own, as it were, and trigger the involuntary actions? It could be repressed emotions, a past trauma, secret sexual urges, or a streak of rebellion otherwise subdued. It could be many things. It occurs when what psychologists call the "supervisory system," that is, the parts of the brain and personality that control behavior, is weakened or distracted. In the extreme, dissociation is the basis for multiple personality disorders.

The person may genuinely feel that he or she is "possessed," but advances in neuroscience offer explanations to counter the religious or mystical interpretations, notes Barry L. Beyerstein, a psychologist at Canada's Simon

Fraser University, who has extensively studied purported paranormal activity.

> Much is going on in the brain simultaneously at all times and when the proceeds of an un-attended mechanism are suddenly served up to the self-aware system, there can be a strong tendency to think that outside manipulation (rather than a semi-autonomous part of our own brains) was responsible. That, after all, is exactly what it feels like at the time.
>
> Because we lack awareness of decisions that are made by operations currently outside the attentional spotlight, we can be mistaken when we try to determine (i.e., consciously, after the fact) why we engaged in some action that seemed to unfold without any sense of having willed or directed it. . . . Given the right cultural and personal background, one readily available answer is that mysterious outside forces must have been pulling the strings.[4]

In addition, much of the behavior that manifests it-self in people who say they are possessed conforms to what the popular culture and the Church have been say-ing for years constitutes demonic interference. In the ex-orcisms I have witnessed or been told about, there is a certain uniformity in the patients' displays. On some unconscious level, a person entering an exorcism may know she is supposed to speak in deep voices and curse at the priest. (Even Linda Blair did it.) While this is not deliberate theatrics necessarily, there is a kind of script.

Dr. Romolo Rossi, a preeminent psychiatrist sometimes described by colleagues as Italy's Freud, says a person who thinks he is possessed often creates in his mind a devil that is a play on his own personality. "You can see the devil as the reverted superego. The demon comes from within us. And who is the demon? He is forged in our style, the style that each of us has within us and lends to the demon. It is not difficult to find in each of us the possibility of evoking this demon, a devil that can come out and show us the contrary of our ideal self."[5]

In addition to hypnosis and autosuggestion, there are other ways to explain almost every aspect of behavior noted during exorcisms and connected to purported demonic possession. Each symptom can be debunked.

Superhuman strength. It is well-known that adrenaline coursing through someone's veins at a moment of stress or crisis can have the effect of producing strength, temporarily, beyond one's normal ability.

Speaking languages the patient cannot know. Critics point out that in many cases, the exorcist does not know the language either. The patient speaks a word or two of another language (not hard to pick up in today's globalized pop culture), which is mixed up with mumbo jumbo, and the priest interprets that as knowledge of a foreign language. In addition, glossolalia, the speaking in tongues normally associated with positive intervention by God rather than by a demon, has been found in some studies to be a kind of rote, rhythmical linguistic code dominated by vowel sounds and playful utterances that can alter the speaker's state of consciousness. It can send the person into a trance.[6] The "languages" spoken by some exorcism patients could be explained along similar lines, although while glossolalia may have a benign, calming effect, the rantings during an exorcism do not.

Aversion to sacred symbols. This can be the classic manifestation of obsessive-compulsive behavior, when, for example, the patient has a seemingly uncontrollable desire to curse in a church. Such actions also feed into the vicious circle that Vincenzo Mastronardi speaks about: to a good Catholic, it is so very unthinkable that he or she would blaspheme the Church or a priest that this becomes confirmation in the person's mind of his or her demonic possession, "self-conviction" instead of recognition of a neurosis. This is also a behavior that is easy to fake, especially when the patient is already going to be aware, on a deeply ingrained level, that lack of respect for religious icons will insult, scandalize, and certainly get attention.

Even Father Dermine, the exorcist, warns against efforts by disturbed people to make themselves the center of attention. "Sometimes resorting to exorcism becomes a way to attract attention from the family and to rehabilitate oneself in the eyes of the family. And so it appears clear in these cases that the patient, pathologically imitating the trance of possession, praises himself with the voice of the devil and in that way proceeds to his own true auto-celebration." It is another reason, as far as Dermine is concerned, to be extremely cautious when offering to perform an exorcism.

Doctors have found that a certain number of people get gratification out of thinking they are possessed, that they have been "chosen," even though it is in a negative sense.

The failure to discern serious illness has led to tragedy and a number of deaths in exorcisms gone awry in the United States—where hundreds of non-Catholic exorcism ministries have sprung up—and Mexico. In 1996 in Los Angeles, for example, a Korean Protestant woman died of beatings in a six-hour exorcism.[7]

In such extreme cases, the actions carried out during the exorcism killed the subject. Of greater frequency is a more insidious problem: the patient, lulled into believing the exorcism is helping and is the appropriate remedy, fails to seek attention for a serious psychological or physiological disease. He allows his sickness to be masked by the supernatural. Within the exorcism, he becomes increasingly convinced that it *is* the devil doing him harm and only the Church can save him. If he is sick he will likely get sicker; his pathological behavior will only worsen. In a few years he could develop schizophrenia or some similar severe mental illness, doctors say.

"I don't think it's crazy. It's worse," University of Florence philosopher Sergio Moravia said. "An exorcism is the residue of a medieval practice completely devoid of any foundation of reason. It's a scam. You promise something to someone who is very sick and at best you offer a temporary cure."

The specter of Italians in a panic over haunted houses, mysteriously moving furniture, and weeping statues of the Madonna became so embarrassing to one group of academics that they formed an organization dedicated to debunking claims of paranormal activity. One of its founders, sociologist Lorenzo Montali, said that in investigating dozens of claims in recent years, he knows of no documented case of paranormal phenomenon. Invariably, he said, the actions (strange sounds, unexplained door closings and light flickerings, objects that appear or disappear) have been made to happen by another person or persons—someone playing a prank or intending to do harm, but always deliberate and at the hands of mortals.

It is not surprising that doctors and intellectuals dismiss the phenomenon of demonic influence as hogwash; what is surprising are those who think it *can* happen. In Catholic Italy, a group of doctors have been recruited into the process and are receptive to the possibility of possession. Science can't explain everything, they say, and in some especially perplexing cases, spiritual therapy may do the patient more good than pharmaceuticals and traditional psychoanalysis.

Among the advocates is Dr. Salvatore di Salvo, a Jungian psychiatrist based in Turin who helped in the training of exorcists for six years until setting the work aside and turning to a new specialty in depression. He believes doctors can help exorcists. In 1989, Cardinal Anastasio Alberto Ballestrero, the now-deceased archbishop of Turin, appointed six exorcists for the city, and he asked doctors like di Salvo to lecture the priests on how to identify signs of psychological disturbance, schizophrenia, and other mental disorders, and how to distinguish such pathologies from "authentic" demonic possession.

More than a decade later, as archbishop of Genoa, Cardinal Tarcisio Bertone established in that city a task force of exorcists and psychiatrists to perform a similar function—to help in the screening of what he described as the huge number of people seeking exorcisms. Their job is to cull out the truly sick as opposed to those in need of a priest. Doctors, Bertone says, can be very valuable in assessing the patient's true state of mind.

"The thinking was that exorcists are often called upon for what are in fact psychiatric disturbances, and it was very important for them to tell the difference. It is very possible to confuse the two," di Salvo said. For example, schizophrenics often suffer from auditory hallucinations—they think they hear voices. And so do people who believe they are possessed. Pointing this out to a po-

tential exorcist presumably prevents him from hastening
to judgment.

At the same time, di Salvo is convinced that there are
events and phenomena that science cannot fully explain,
and that only the "arrogance of science" insists it must.
Scientists must open their minds to the possibility of demonic possession, di Salvo argues, while priests must sus-
pend the idea that the devil is lurking behind any and all
trouble. For some patients, it makes sense to see both an
exorcist and a psychiatrist, he said. "Medicine will act
only on the psychological disturbance, and at the same
time the exorcism will work only on the demonic presence. It doesn't make it worse."

The priests that he lectured did not always listen to
him. Di Salvo recalled one exorcist who told his patient
that the medicine his psychiatrist had prescribed was "the
devil's drug"; the patient stopped taking it. Several of the
exorcists were pretty strong-minded and had their own
ideas about what to do. Still, di Salvo approved of the
exercise, and he has nothing but praise for the attitude
and methods of Father Amorth, whom he credits with
bringing exorcism "out of the shadows." Amorth has
maintained regular contact with di Salvo and other psychiatrists for years.

Academic Massimo Introvigne, the alternative religions expert, is another advocate. He cautions against ex-
aggerating the threat of satanic cults and favors science
over fundamentalism, but "as a Catholic" he too believes

in demonic possession as a possibility and sees an important role to be played by the exorcist.

"Bad exorcists are too gullible, but most are quite good and can offer counseling," he said. The vast majority of people seeking exorcisms do not need them, he noted, but if the Church does not address the demand and provide these people with an exorcist, at least to listen and steer them in the right direction, then they might turn to charlatans, psychics, and practitioners of the occult. "And that would cause serious damage," he said.

For the most devout of Catholics, belief in demons and exorcism may be the ultimate evidence of faith. But if the numbers offered by the Italian Association of Psychiatrists and Psychologists—that thousands of Italians seek exorcisms annually—are anywhere near the truth, then far too many people are turning to a procedure that even many priests say should be the course of last resort. The extent to which some members of the clergy fuel this form of supernatural hysteria is worrisome.

Some psychiatrists suggest there can be a temporary placebo effect in a mild exorcism that in the short term could help the patient. It is the long-term addiction to exorcism that has the potential for greater harm.

The most troubling aspect of this story of exorcists and their exorcisms is the patients. Caterina, the dancer, perhaps gets comfort and strength from her weekly sessions with her exorcist, and that enables her to live a workaday life. Enza, the troubled woman who goes to

Bishop Gemma, is deeply disturbed and does not appear to be receiving the help she needs. Francesca, the doctor, has, at least for now, returned to her profession as a doctor in a hospital and seems to be functioning.

Humankind will forever need to grapple with evil, confront horrors, and cope with tragedy. The limits and definitions of human understanding are always expanding. Modern society will continue to search for ways to reconcile faith and knowledge.

As Lorenzo Montali, the sociologist, put it, it's important to keep an open mind. But not so open that our brains fall out.

EPILOGUE

As I was finishing this book, Father Amorth popped up in public again, after a lull of several months. He was speaking at a religious conference—and getting himself in trouble one more time. Interviewed on the official Vatican Radio, he repeated his conviction that exorcism is a valuable tool for fighting the devil and evil, especially in those rare cases of demonic possession. Asked by the Vatican Radio reporter whether people can really be possessed by the devil, he was definitive. "The devil can possess not only single individuals but also groups and entire populations," he said. "For example, I am convinced that the Nazis were all possessed by the devil. If one thinks of what was committed by people like Stalin [or] Hitler . . . certainly they were possessed by the devil. This is seen in their actions, in their behavior and in the horrors that they committed or ordered to be committed."

The comments drew angry reactions from Jewish groups as well as a number of Catholic theologians, who saw the attempt to blame the world's most egregious atrocities on the devil as a cop-out that removes the element of personal responsibility. Citing demonic possession essentially lets evildoers off the hook. Some officials in the Church, similarly, have referred to the sex-abuse scandals plaguing the priesthood as a case of "the smoke of Satan" infecting the clergy. When the late pope John Paul II finally broke his stubborn silence on the matter, he invoked the central Catholic tenet on the power of evil to corrupt, saying that a number of priests had succumbed to supernatural evil, "the most grievous forms of *mysterium iniquitatis* [Latin for "mystery of evil"] at work in the world."

For outsiders, such assertions raise questions of credibility for the Church, and of accountability.

Exorcisms raise similar questions. The tales recounted in these pages are presumably believed by the people who told them. It remains a dubious assertion, to me at least, that exorcisms provide true curative relief. That is not the same as saying that prayer has no power to heal. Again, the mind plays an indispensable role.

What is the future of exorcism in Italy, headquarters of the Roman Catholic Church?

Pope Benedict XVI has praised the exorcists, and his predecessor performed exorcisms. But in the second year of his papacy, the former Joseph Ratzinger is also stressing the importance of injecting reason into faith. Reason without faith and a belief in the mystery of God is dangerous, he says. But so is a faith that excludes reason. It can lead to fanaticism, even violence.

That may be the cautionary message that more exorcists, and their parishioners, should heed. In contrast to the enthusiasm of Amorth and other exorcists, members of the Church hierarchy evince a far more tepid acceptance. Most psychiatrists condemn the practice, yet others, along with a number of academics, see it as useful. With the rise, here and elsewhere, of Christian fundamentalism, unorthodox interpretations of faith, and rampant, confused uncertainty among the public, it seems likely priests will continue to exorcise and, even more so, believers will seek them.

Says Amorth, "There is still a generalized resistance in the clergy, even now. I think they are afraid. But priests, young and old, are coming to me to learn, so I see the number of exorcists continuing to grow. I think the future is secure."

Notes

Prologue

This section is based on interviews with Father Efrem Cirlini and his superiors, as well as with Caterina, whose real name I agreed not to publish. Primarily, the section describes an exorcism that my colleague, Maria de Cristofaro, and I witnessed in Bologna in the summer of 2005.

Chapter I: Introduction

1. Blatty, *The Exorcist*, p. 190.

Chapter II: Overview

Much of the information in this chapter, especially the descriptions of the ritual, the process of determining its necessity, the categories of demonic influence, and so forth, come from my interviews with Amorth and numerous other exorcists, as well as from their public lectures and writings. See also articles by John L. Allen Jr. of the *National Catholic Reporter*, who wrote extensively in 2000 about the growth of exorcism and the role of the Charismatic movement.

1. Harris Poll, Dec. 14, 2005. See www.harrisinteractive .com, poll no. 90.

2. For more on the Catholic Charismatic movement, see Cuneo, *American Exorcism*, chapters 7–10.

3. The Catholic Church opposes assisted fertility because embryos are sometimes destroyed in the process.

4. I developed the background on canonizations and specifically on the cause involving Mother Teresa and Monica Besra in the course of research for several *Los Angeles Times* articles in 2003. The research included interviews with Fathers Peter Gumpel and Robert J. Sarno, priests with the Congregation for the Causes of Saints, the Vatican department that handles the naming of saints; and with Father Brian Kolodiejchuk, the promoter of Mother Teresa's cause. For more on the process, see Woodward's *Making Saints*.

5. Moravia, interview with the author for an article in the *Los Angeles Times*, 2004.

6. Catechism of the Catholic Church, No. 1673.

7. Ibid.

8. Taken from the Roman Ritual, with translation from the Latin by Pietro de Cristofaro.

9. From Amorth's *An Exorcist: More Stories*, p. 12.

CHAPTER III: HISTORY

1. Many of these translations are cited in *The Westminster Dictionary of Christian Theology*, eds. Richardson and Bowden, pp. 150, 521, in McBrien's *Catholicism*, p. 1125, and elsewhere.

2. Pope Cornelius's letter is mentioned in many places, including John Allen's articles.

3. Russell, essay in *The Westminster Dictionary of Christian Theology*, eds. Richardson and Bowden, p. 150.

4. For discussion of views of Satan in historical texts, see Wray and Mobley, *The Birth of Satan*.

5. Menghi and Paxia, *The Devil's Scourge*.

6. Amorth, *An Exorcist Tells His Story*, p. 61.

7. Tanner, interview with author.

8. Catechism of the Catholic Church, No. 395.

9. The text of Paul VI's general audience, like all official speeches and statements of the popes, can be found on the official Vatican Web site, www.vatican.va.

10. Magister's accounts are collected on his Web site, www.chiesa.espressonline.it. John Allen identified the woman in the 1982 exorcism as Francesca Fabrizzi.

11. Medina was seen by international audiences when, in his role as senior deacon, he stepped onto the balcony over Saint Peter's Square in April 2005 to announce the election of the new pope. It was Medina who intoned the words: "Habeamus papum."

12. Medina's comments are from an interview with the author in early 2005 and from a 1999 press conference at which he presented the revised rite.

13. In the summer of 2006, Pope Benedict appointed

Bertone as his new secretary of state, the second highest position at the Vatican.

14. O'Collins's interview with the author.
15. John Paul II's World Day of Peace message, like all his speeches, can be found on the official Vatican Web site, www.vatican.va.

Chapter IV: The Exorcists

1. The Legionaries' Mexican founder, Father Marcial Maciel, was forced to step down in 2005 after he was accused of sexually molesting seminarians, a charge he vigorously denied. In the spring of 2006, Maciel was censured by the Vatican as a result of its investigation into the allegations; the elderly priest was ordered to refrain from public ministries and to live a life of "prayer and penitence."
2. Associated Press, Washington, D.C., July 13, 2006.

Chapter V: Patients

For history of the witch hunts, see Demos, *Entertaining Satan*, and Levack, *The Witch-Hunt in Early Modern Europe*.

Francesca's story, including the details of her ailments and her treatment, is completely her own recollection. Some pieces of the story could be verified with her psychiatrist. It was also verifiable that she worked for Milingo, in whose offices we first encountered her.

Chapter VI: Satanic Cults

Much of the discussion of the Beasts of Satan is based on extensive journalistic coverage in the Italian press, including articles in the Milan daily *Corriere della Sera*, the Rome newspaper *La Repubblica*, and Turin's *La Stampa*, as well as from the national news agency, Ansa. The protagonists also gave numerous television interviews. In addition, many of the facts were recounted in interviews I conducted with experts, including Massimo Introvigne, who specializes in alternative religions; Father Aldo Buonaiuto, who has maintained a counseling relationship with one of the convicted members of the Beasts of Satan gang; and a forensic archaeologist who worked on the case and who asked to remain anonymous because of his sensitive role.

1. Eurispes, "Il Buio oltre l'occulto," from Italy Report 2002.
2. Guerrieri's story and his version of events were told to Buonaiuto, who recounted them in an interview.
3. "Sects, Brainwashing and Crime: Case Studies," prepared by Italian police for the International Crime Analysis Association, 2005.

Chapter VII: Divergence Within the Church

1. The Groeschel forward is in Amorth's *An Exorcist Tells His Story*, pp. 7–8.
2. Cuneo on Groeschel in *American Exorcism*, pp. 40–41.

Chapter VIII: Skeptics and Shrinks

The ideas and information in this chapter come largely from the writings of and my interviews with psychiatrists, psychologists, and academics—those cited and also Dr. Scott Lilienfeld, a professor of psychology at Emory University in Atlanta, Georgia. See also Spanos, *Multiple Identities and False Memories*.

1. Leland E. Hinsie, et. al., *Psychiatric Dictionary* (London, Oxford University Press, 1940).
2. Vincenzo Mastronardi, in a paper and speech to the 11th annual congress of the Italian Society of Psychopathology, Rome, February 2006; also in an interview with the author.
3. Ari Kiev, "Primitive Religious Rites and Behavior: Clinical Considerations," in *Clinical Psychiatry and Religion*, ed. Pattison, pp. 119–131.
4. Barry L. Beyerstein, "Dissociative States: Possession and Exorcism," in *The Encyclopedia of the Paranormal*, ed. Gordon Stein.
5. Rossi, in a paper and speech to the 11th annual congress of the Italian Society of Psychopathology, Rome, February 2006.
6. E. Mansell Pattison and Robert L. Casey, "Glossolalia: A Contemporary Mystical Experience," in *Clinical Psychiatry and Religion*, ed. Pattison, pp. 133–48.
7. *Los Angeles Times*, "Ritual Ends in Death," July 6, 1996; and "Judge Rules Exorcism Death Manslaughter," April 17, 1997.

BIBLIOGRAPHY

Amorth, Gabriele. *An Exorcist Tells His Story*. San Francisco: Ignatius Press, 1999.

——. *An Exorcist: More Stories*. San Francisco: Ignatius Press, 2002.

Bamonte, Francesco. *Occult, Christianity and Magic*. Chawton, England: Many Rooms Publishing, 2001.

Beyerstein, Barry L. "Dissociative States: Possession and Exorcism." In *Encyclopedia of the Paranormal*, edited by Gordon Stein. Buffalo, NY: Prometheus Books, 1995.

——. "Neuropathology and the Legacy of Spiritual Possession." In *The Skeptical Inquirer*. CSICOP. Spring, 1988.

Blatty, William Peter. *The Exorcist*. London: Corgi Books, 1972.

Buonaiuto, Aldo. *Le Mani Occulte: Viaggio nel mondo del satanismo*. Rome: Citta Nuova Editrice, 2005.

Catechism of the Catholic Church. 2nd ed. Doubleday, 1995.

Cuneo, Michael W. *American Exorcism: Expelling Demons in the Land of Plenty.* London: Bantam Books, 2002.

Demos, John. *Entertaining Satan: Witchcraft and the Culture of Early New England.* New York: Oxford University Press, 1983.

Esorcismo e preghiera di liberazion: Atti del corso. Rome: Edizioni Art, 2005.

Ferrari, Giuseppe, et al. *Il Fenomeno del Satanismo Nella Societa Contemporanea.* Vatican City: L'Osservatore Romano, 1997.

Fiori, Moreno. *Satanismo e Sette Religiose.* Montespertoli, Italy: Aleph Edizioni, 2000.

————. *Il Maleficio: Indagine sulle pratiche del male.* Rome: Citta Nuova Editrice, 2005.

The Holy Bible, Revised Standard Version. Meridian Books, 1962.

Levack, Brian. *The Witch-Hunt in Early Modern Europe.* New York: Longman, 1995.

Martin, Malachi. *Hostage to the Devil: The Possession and Exorcism of Five Living Americans.* San Francisco: HarperSanFrancisco, 1992 (1976).

McBrien, Richard P. *Catholicism.* New York: Harper-Collins, 1994.

Menghi, Girolamo, and Gaetano Paxia. *The Devil's Scourge: During the Italian Renaissance.* Boston: Weiser Books, 2002.

O'Collins, Gerald, and Mario Farrugia. *Catholicism: The*

Story of Catholic Christianity. Oxford: Oxford University Press, 2003.

Pattison, E. Mansell, M.D., *Clinical Psychiatry and Religion*. Boston: Little, Brown and Company, 1969.

Peck, M. Scott, M.D. *Glimpses of the Devil: A Psychiatrist's Personal Accounts of Possession, Exorcism and Redemption*. New York: Free Press, 2005.

Richardson, Alan, and John Bowden, eds. *The Westminster Dictionary of Christian Theology*. Philadelphia: Westminster Press, 1983.

Rituale Romanum: De Exorcismis et Supplicationibus Quibusdam. Amended version. Vatican City: Libreria Editrice Vaticana, 2004.

Russell, Jeffrey Burton. *The Devil: Perceptions of Evil from Antiquity to Primitive Christianity*. Ithaca, NY: Cornell University Press, 1977.

———. *Satan: The Early Christian Tradition*. Ithaca, NY: Cornell University Press, 1981.

Spanos, Nicholas P. *Multiple Identities and False Memories: A Sociocognitive Perspective*. Washington: American Psychological Association, 1996.

Woodward, Kenneth L. *Making Saints: How the Catholic Church Determines Who Becomes a Saint, Who Doesn't, and Why*. New York: Touchstone, 1990.

Wray, T. J., and Gregory Mobley. *The Birth of Satan: Tracing the Devil's Biblical Roots*. New York: Palgrave Macmillan, 2005.

İ ⊓ D E X

Index

Index

Index

Revelation
12:3-4, 36
12:9, 63
rites of cleansing, 22–23, 69–70
rite of exorcism, revision ("De
exorcismus et
Supplicationibus
Quibusdam"), 49–52, 83,
145–46
Roman Catholic Church
ambivalent attitudes toward
demonic possession and
exorcism, 143–49
canonization of saints, miracle
requirement, 13–15, 170n.
4
Congregation for Divine
Worship, 8, 50, 145–46
Congregation for the Causes
of Saints, 170n. 4
Congregation for the Doctrine
of the Faith, 52
controversy on the nature of
evil and the devil, 3, 53–55
controversy over Emmanuel
Milingo, 86–87, 97, 145
exorcism in church history,
33–56
future of exorcism and,
166–67
membership size, 10
positions on evil, 46–47
positions on Satan, 44
power of prayer and, 13
Reformation and, 37
revision of exorcism rite ("De
exorcismus et
Supplicationibus

Quibusdam"), 49–52, 83,
145–46
rules for exorcism, 3–4, 16, 24,
28–29, 41–42, 49–52, 60, 83,
145
rules for healing ceremonies,
51, 94
Sacra Romana Rota, 61
sanctioning of exorcisms, xiv,
1, 52–53, 60, 97, 144–45
Second Vatican Council
reforms, 12, 45–46, 147
Vatican and exorcism, 3, 8
Vatican Web site, 171n. 9,
172n. 15
Roman Ritual (Rituale
Romanum), 28–29, 46
Romans 8:28, 45
Rossi, Romolo, 157
Ruggieri, Pier Domenico, 126–28
Russell, Jeffrey Burton, 34

S

saints. *See also specific saints*
called upon, during exorcisms,
xvi
canonization, miracle
requirement, 13–15, 170n.
4
salt, holy, used for protection,
106, 109
Santa Maria Auxiliatrice, Genoa,
53
Santa Scala Church, Rome, 48
Ss. [Santi] Gregoria e Siro
Church, Bologna, xiv
Santi Silvestro e Martino ai Monti
Church, Rome, 104
Sarno, Father Robert J., 170n. 4

187

Satan. *See* devil (Satan)
satanic cults, 19, 27, 58, 121–22,
        129–49, 162, 173n
    Bambini de Satana, 72, 135
    Beasts of Satan, 129–32,
        133–34, 135, 137–39,
        173n
    law enforcement perspective,
        140–42
    priests and counseling for
        members, 136–39
Society of Saint Paul, Rome, 11,
        21, 22
Socio-Religious Research and
        Information Group, 59
Strano, Marco, 140–42
Sung, Marie, 86–87

T
Tanner, Father Norman, 44,
        148–49
Taraborelli, Father Vincenzo,
        103–5
Teresa of Calcutta, Mother,
        14–15, 170n. 4
Thomas Aquinas, Saint, 40
1 Timothy 2:13-14, 98–99
Todi, Italy, 8
Tollis, Fabio, 130–31, 138, 139
Turin, Italy, 59, 102, 161

U
United States
    American Pentacostals in, 9
    death from exorcism in, 159
    exorcisms in, 159
    belief in hell, 9
    belief in incarnate evil, 9
    interest in exorcism, 47
    witch hunts in, 100
Urban VIII, Pope, 42

V
Venice, Italy, 81, 82
Viadana, Italy, 39
Volpe, Andrea, 130–32

W
women. *See also* patients
        (exorcism cases)
    assisting in exorcism, 8
    devil working through, 99
    as focus of evil, 98–99
    in Islam, 99
    seeking exorcism, versus men,
        98, 101
    witches or witchcraft and,
        100, 172n

Z
Zagarolo, Italy, 87–89, 122, 124